A World Of Nothing But Nations

a book of Strophaics

Tod Thilleman

hivepress

New York City
1999

Some of these strophes, in a different arrangement
appeared in *Antenym*, *The Cafe Review*, *Lingo* (VA.), *Lyric&* and *Yefief*.

cover art: The Lorenz Attractor and its X, Y and Z breakdown.

ISBN 0 - 9661254 - 0 - 1

Hive Press
3 West 102 Street 5b
NYC 10025
Upsidehive@bigfoot.com

Library of Congress Cataloging-in-Publication Data

Thilleman, Tod.
A world of nothing but nations: a book of strophaics/ Tod Thilleman

     p. cm.
  ISBN 0-9661254-0-1
  I. Title
  PS3570.H453W67   1998
  811'. 54--dc21   97-52943
                      CIP

Foreword

Part of a 300 notebook project aimed at constructing a pseudoscience, these *Strophaics* allude to Being and Existence in general, lyricism as Ontic resonance, and structure as adjunct to a consumer-based industrialism. Each "level" is constructed from 10 notebooks. All the strophes here were cut from the 10, separated into a shoebox, 300 then blindly chosen for their present order.

Events were jotted down by the poet into a tiny pocket-sized notebook at the moment of encounter. Because of that the pieces here are perceived as connected circuitry, regardless of their chronological tones: over-tone and under-tone have traded places and the result, of course, matters little at the level of appearance, the performative or percussive. The poem gives an impression of atemporality since all of its elements are sifted through the immediately present. There is a *déjà vu preponderance*, whether looked into performatively, textually, or empirically.

This is a quantitative verse, but it's not quantitative to linear scansion. All structure is evolving around a mental circuitry creating a heightened state of dèjá vu.

It does not matter how you read this poem (you can start at the end and continue toward the first page, or in the middle out toward beginning or end) the experience will always be complete and yet somehow different for each reader. The physical arrangement of the lines is not relevant thus symbolizing visually a mosaic, the prototype for the "workings" of the human brain (cf. *The Cerebral Code* by William H. Calvin.) Every minuscule part contains the whole. (cf. *Chaos and Fractals* by Pietgen, Jurgens, and Saupe.)

The poem can be described as nonlinear but this non-linearity is not created by any technological innovation (hypertext, etc.). Through the reader's personal allusions and independent of technology, the poet has used spontaneity to convey the complexity of experience by scrutinizing the fibers of the immediate. That is, since everything in the poem occurs in the present it requires the reader to be tense, to construct and dis-assemble complex mental connections. The whole poem's syntagem will never settle in so-called perception alone, allowing for a never-ending mental *activity* in its every evolution.

The structure as strophe, a simple quantitative factor, organized around replicating parts. This skeleton is deceiving, however, since it relies on its own generation of meaning. In that sense the poem is no longer a solid structure but instead resembles DNA. The Strophe is not an ossified construct here but a figuration that can support flexibility and mutation. It is a repetitive unit, sure, but it is rather a form than a formula, and it *con*-forms to our notion about systems, that is, they *evolve*. We live in an open world where, among other things, texts and their interpretations are never final.

Tod Thilleman bases his *Strophaic* work around the verse form of Alloestrophaed measure, a form exploited by Milton, among others. Milton, in turn, borrowed it from the Greeks who used this structure in their epic drama as a dance and choral element. Milton accomplished an internalization of the chorus to enlarge his subject. It's a blank verse—there's no rhyme structure carried to an alienating extreme.

Another element of the poem not to be ignored is the departure from a cause/effect tug-of-war. Instead, there is a sustained entrance to the incontestable domain of inter-subjectivity. *Inter-subjective frames* situated in reality appear throughout the poem. Inter-subjectivity, of course, is an alternative to scientific objectivity creating a conceptual unity within modernity. Technically, "inter-subjectivity" and "objectivity" have been given the same meaning, but inter-subjectivity focuses a human factor upon the possibility of unified perspective by an emotive Being. Objectivity precludes some kind of agreement between machinery, denying the validity of the emotive character of man. In fact, this foregrounding of inter-subjectivity proposes a new world perception where understanding channels through shifting networks similar to our highly complex nervous system. It is an understanding of homeostasis as THE center to sanity.

The voice in the poem is, finally, that that transmits through a machine, not because of a machine. This differs from most contemporary American Poetry obsessed with biographical detail. Here is a collection, then, molding an integration of the postmodern into contemporary vision.

Hive Press
NYC 1999

for EKSTONISTIAN
leader of insurgency

LEVEL ONE:
Toward An Ontology

The Master Architect has arranged horizons in a renewing design.

Robert Duncan
"Stimmung"

Modern empiricism
seeks to contain
celestial regions
harness their power and knowledge
and chain the aspirations of man
into reason's judgement
     "Why is it so easy to misinterpret chemical and phys-
ical occurrences with the process that is being accomplished?
These conversations remind me of the old man who tore apart
a radio to observe the transistors and studied them for years
until someone finally told him it was not the tool that made the
music it was the artist."
     All I do is
sit around the house
sit around the job
from which my body aches
     I thought
that if I wound myself up
I'd not be left behind
     You will never find
a better advocate
to bourgeois values
than the long-enduring
proletariat member

they love the frippery
the foppery, the system
that is more mind, than system
          From here out
to the chaos of the bounds
of peopled black & white
where will meet with
constipation and the sway
withering an ungoverned inclination
            "...Only if these drives are..."
wind thru the seed pods
wind-chimes tinkling
I am writing
my eyes blinking
notebook held in palm's crease
sound of the world outside this room's hum
          A tin can, birds
          The sun's
an opened window
opened it
the sun on beaded
water
          Brass door-stop
dotted the floor
black grout
reflected in sink-stand's leg
a glass breaks
the register rings
I'm doing lines in the bathroom
a towel on the edge
of the grey waste basket
          Give me a cigarette then
          Red glow
in the form of a question
bass filling my ear
the end is near
          I know that it is me

in the shadow
the table's leg casts
under it to where
the cat's pillow's worn
in a dark place
beyond description
animal-kind
       Girl, you don't realize
all of what is fading
away
       Streaming
idling is a name
to use to fill
up the, this
time
       Nose piece
and the singer
eyes dart
"What happened here...."
tea cup, book closed
cookie in my wife's mouth
lower teeth
and a tone
       In the bathroom
after the reading
what did Fitz mean
when he asked me
about my wife, saying
I used to be
something a skirt-chaser
something like that
but now the paper's run out of space
       We don't know
but we're gonna find out
what poetry was, and
is, and, what's the difference?
       I needed

order, even if it's
artificial, and so
found mosaic
and my attachment
is such
as to transpose into nature
   Identity so easily
takes the center
magnetized and magnetizing
   Gasping and dropping onto it
a little urchin with spikes
and so he figures now to open
to pry out the food cupped within
and tastes the cool salty dollop
and hears chords of bright music
ranging the wastes of home
   How grows that
girl's face
she wants
to look
   Looking for rest
he's found it the table
rocking from my body a bird
it squeaks the wind the sound
squeals high-pitched
wind with it now a fiction
conceit curls in my mind
the coffee glints and I hear
   Right outside my window
all the serendipitous traffic
what was it drew me in
clothing all forms
with that appeal
   It's gonna be a poet
tells you all you've
we have
lost

Banana stems
blackly mottled
the print on the coffee cup
phone number
stove front
smoke
wrinkled clear plastic
"...iqui...tors"
"On January 28"
pen clinks, thrown
            Word's meaning itself
a serendipitous energy
assigned to all space
all time, all products thereof
and everything else besides
            "The small consolation prize"
Footsteps, hum
paused arm held
creaking wood
"Should we wash our bedsheets?"
            "What is it that they do
...and have we not
frailty as men have?"
            Maybe there is never any separation
and that all at once it happens
but then why the dying tread
of its life into the sodden
flesh as a muted inevitability
driven away by spells
its spell's in control of
or this is all wrong
            Time distinguishes
what is practical
and what is not
in man's world
            I know everything
about it

all around it
thru it
and the sides
and how it comes
out in a form
that is it
                Is there belief
beyond knowing
                The metonymic character of realism
mediates the two realms
                Light reflected
in the black window
"red azalea"
"...special performance..."
looking as the book falls
and I scratched my shoulder
"...directions being directed..."
                Squeaking
and cruise now
clacking, a circle
squeaking and a rise
of turbulence
                "Language really exists
only when a speaker takes it
in his possession and actualizes it.
But at the same time as the event
of discourse is fleeting and transitory,
it can be identified as 'the same';
thus, meaning is introduced, in its broadest sense,
at the same time as the possibility
of identifying a given unit of discourse."
                A jet just went thru my ear
                Now we're
getting somewhere
one whole
year
later

Sad dog's nose in grass
I want to be
so inspired
that I
will burst
into
You're not gonna
get anywhere
without a quantifiable verse
so just stop right there
think, what place
does that or this
have in common with calculation
we do not know
What, in the mind
has a pipeline
to the cover-up
of nakidity
Cigarettes
and an astro attacker
It is the opposition
of what this is
that determines this
and these entries
Wind thru the trees
jet sound
belch
wind in the pods
cat leaps to chair, fixed
headache
"Intuition"
she licks
Inscribed with
the expected
Not just a momentary
gathering of one's energy
to grunt out another turd

but the whole project
fragmentation's opened up
by an over-importation
of non-poetic centers
of so-called pertinence
            "...the trope truly does consist
OF one word; however, if one may speak in this manner,
it occurs between two ideas,
by transfer from one to the other. Hence,
in a sense that will have to be clarified,
the trope, like epiphora before it,
occurs 'based upon a duality' (see above, page 25)."
            Neither devil
nor man
I'm mortal
            Cacophonous voices
for a long time
            Spoon off the edge
underneath are crumbs
a light from the opening door
bursts into this diner
where the silver-ware
and voices keep talking
about something
            Gun, lines, gun
headband
blue lines
remote control
voices trapped me
            Spearing fish
            Ripping off
a long stream
of toilet paper
            Do not hope, you hope in vain
for human reason
to take up your curse
your push thru the clouds

this you must do alone
till you curse their very
existence, and only then
              "...to thus characterize
poems trivializes
the whole poetic process."
              The pit of sound
attacks to the habit
and becomes a face
where dark black
outlines
serve to trace it
and repair it
              I have passed this
world thru
and sits in contemplation
the pure perfect rumbling
cloud-strewn covenant
of flash and mysterious
undaunted presence
              The burden is buckets
on backs and in stomachs
buckets of wind
the doctorate in cap and gowns
toothless and hoary
bitter and frail
              I mean
how long
can you hold your breath
              We have resolved
to write no
event that hasn't
happened
              Her jaw's moving
              Mike-stands, knees
and cymbals gathering
all the force

a crystal candle yellow
red glow over the
bass yells
mouth black tonsils
      I got a bunch of ideas
but hold on, Tim
they're falling into place
from between my intents
for the purpose of plays
and all that might bring us
      I thought that if the
head were not dignified
belabored in that thought
then value had no name
and time needed throwing away
today I know, that short
unbecoming pang, identifies
the hand fanning toward me, my only dread
      We have laid down our life
between a sword and a sword
for peace
for the extermination of us
we have heaped our conceits
gabbing at the gates of dawn
that we cannot rend open to enter
      Looking for the way
      I, poet, belong
and yet do not
having been cast out, and
forever doomed to wander
set my tent in what IS a desert
knowing no return but my own approaching death
      What would ever happen
but war outside love
      The soft gelid urge
of the pliant vitamin
muscled and greased limbs

moving into light
obscured by soot and mortality
slow breathing in a bastion of sound
      "Yet the red sun and moon,
and all the overflowing stars
rain down prolific pains"
      What's in my mind
is the future and past
of humanity
wheezing thru gooey
contingency
      You better believe it
entire world
conspiring to manipulate
that penny whistle
      "Just watch his route here..."
      "There are powers"
the radio, "Bradley...
congressional...how much...
by the way...congress...
you may retire wealthy...
generous...corporations...
examining congress's pension plan."
      Mighty thought
rises on the stem of power
      The searing circle
of the fire
within which
bodies stand
caught in a fiction
like aliens
      Is your mind there
to un-translate
the terror of this race?
      Gene fragments
      Mankind is weeping
muscles vibrating in his sadness

a simple pink sadness
painted flesh, eyes
opening to the light surrounding
enveloping brief moments
as he plummets again into dread
          "It"
is this
thing I
bend or bends me
through ITS
warp
          It's my own self's
my own enemy
          Now the engine
stops and hums
as the space grows
and the head glows
I can see it
what a miracle
what is happening?
          Held within the thrall
of imagination
there is nothing else
modernism's mistaken identity
a classical evolution
graces the world
          What wanted
more to open
open wide to see
and be among now
seems in being but
the deepest hollowed depth of
love's wet thirst in
endless here-ness
          Something
scraped off
in, deep in the bowel

to show what motion
what release and everything to echo off of
forever and ever
          Word's approximation-orbit
substantiality's new man
          Sentience:
marginal societies
viewed as inclusive
of the category
you're controlled by
its extensions all the way
thru the center of town
          Eventually
the sun gains center-stage
          Why should I, be yet another
to choose between speech modality
or langue-lexical writing
as the mode for what will ultimately become
an aesthetic sound-byte buried in the so-called brain
of subsequent man
          Man's empiricism
is a near-sighted means
to a far-sighted
much unknown goal
          What is it about prediction
that zings the sentence along
          One of my life's great lessons:
early '70's, Orson Welles
on the Dinah Shore show
she says: "Oh you must like
Happy Days! We do!" as the
audience applauds. He says:
"How many here like Bozo's circus?"
and the same crowd applauds and cheers.
          "What do you mean"
          Notes
struck by the strophaic

echo all man's learning
and the aspirations thereof
      Where the bait is
they all gather like fleas
to attack the blood of characterization
and all possible characterizations
      Please, who ever
can hear me
move
out of the city
go work in the country
to ballast the free side
what's left, of humanity
too late?
      "This would endanger the possibility
of conceiving the interference required
by the very thesis that aporetic ontology
takes its perspective from unitary theology.
I should even be tempted to see,
in these arguments that tend to make this interference
unintelligible at the very moment it is, alleged,
the profound reason that led Aristotle's successors,
and perhaps even Aristotle himself, to appeal to analogy."
      I don't want you
to be swayed
by what I believe
      "Is that ok?"
      How, again
was I to use my time
the time, be with time
correctly?
      A horn, or strings
sonorous
in and out
      "Mrs. Hinkley
are you insane?"
giggles, giggles

"No further questions"
Salacious leg openings
"Perjury is a serious offense"
"They all know she's the murderer"
   Trying, to satisfy
the rhythm at its center
   "Editorial
letters
books
bog report
outings"
   Leibniz and then
also Spinoza
monads and modes
"windowless cells"
said W. Lewis
they are already interlocked
in not being unified by Whitehead
and are called "Reality"
   The manifestoed rain
still falls upon the lowly people
seeding their future mad
dictator's murderous pace
   Now
upon my return
searching
and releasing
not finding
what it was/
is, unless it's this
   Whole place of "zap"
when I look at
printed matter
   Beat, chimes, lines
3 of those each one
I would want
to echo

the incredible sound
overpowering the air
          Cat-eyes
in the dark brow
          You are not
going back in memory
you're going back
to the past
what it was, specifically
what it was as
something that is
          Enough energy
to pronounce it
needed, yes, but what
about those times
we indicate by "thought"
have rendered
all wheels to speed
          Even under hypnosis
I'd still succumb
to this romance
where the leg of the table
and the wobbling radio
and the cat picking the window
frame, intrudes where I
          I am simply
not interested
in being known
          Trying to find myself
thru the shifting stuff
of and on the mind of me
          Coffee cup with brown line
around its white center
a little handle like an ear
a gleam on a saucer
creamer pointed away
from me, a small cup with

sugar leafed out its top
       What MAN threatened you
but THE man, big and burly
scary potential of violence
       Eventually, all this thinking does
is produce psychic stings that
find a way toward him
to mean him and de-mean
       Plastic sibilance
       The talking on the phone
cigarette ash
when I look
"...flaky..."
       A dream is something you live
but do not know
do not know to live
but it moves in and lives
for you, perhaps
but you become
awake to it over time
       I think you'll find
that bourgeois decorum
knows no class distinction
       The empty NO upon
a mountain of dirt
where one spies
and ground an arrow
thru the logic of
while other life goes on
outside the tincture of droplets
       Flattened out
between horizon's land
and sky
a certain science to it
       The earth's dark
force field
       The impressions of the letters

on the writing pad
sirens and the door closed
the refrigerator operates
and a decibel range
configures all this room
   What am I searching for
   "Now just a plain old
category one hurricane"
   You could
write an endless poem
main character
of a narrative
whose name's "where"
and all the events
it witnesses
   It is life-thrilling
to not see
thread's way
propinquity
   Out of ordinary scenes
of wall and street
come voices and stars
the shape of heart's
preponderance
haloed in dull endless space
   "If there is a point in our experience
where living expression states
living existence, it is where our
movement up the entropic slope
of language
encounters the movement
by which we come back
this side of distinctions
between actuality,
action, production,
motion."
   This, again

a beat
sustaining air of
words a-light from
back into deep meaning's well
the deep black
endless pit identity's
sucked into and covered by
       What age is this
should be aware of
tho its progress
would elude me also?
       Footsteps on wood floor
hair delicately annoying
a drawer slides
the radio is talking
'a' not 'o'
hair tickles the nose-flange
       I am guilty
for going against
myself, everything
I would have otherwise
set myself to do
and yet I see no other way
but this in which to thrive
       Eye lights open, moves
when all's forgotten
       Mind shows us
that man comes from nothing
from his belly
and that his development
belongs to the development
of man and not to the
development
of mind, tho it will
claim it as its own by some
       It is true
things stick to you

and for release
there is always
political rant
      Via negativa
is called the way
called away
to duty
today
      At the possible confluence
the moist exciting
part of the game
      He doubles over in a vain exercise
to demand it all make sense, now
      Kite flies high
      Wings of separate color
stained-glass wire mesh
veins of straight
cubes dark and big wood
one square a mouth
a mustache of leaves
with two lead points
      Smoke rising up
from the just
lit
cigarette
      Half-shells
light & shadows
chord change
ink marks soaring
muscles of left leg
free to rhythm
gears chromatic yowls
      The ferns lay
on the sand
and have died
embedded make a print
and the black storm

off in the distance
        Only one place
point between the eyes
matters, ultimately
about anything
hovers there
that place
remains as long as
anything that is
        "Honest to Pete"
        Empiricism
still munching
at the mythic biscuit
        Upon this height
where the look and fell
goes down into the world
we fear to enter
and stand here
stamping our place with feet
never meant to go further
        It looks like an eye
in the distance
collapsing
        Standing
in the middle
of tiles my eye sees
as the water begins to boil
and the stove's flame
bursts
I have a blue vest
        "Memo"
ashtray with 2 butts
folds of
cat falls off cushion
rain drops and pings of ice
pen, not my usual
the sound of the refrigerator

Nothing more heart-wrenching
than watching those about you
go to work for
a cure for death
            "The magazine
that speaks for animals"
            Car wheels rotating
wet pavement
and a tumbling chassis
and a sound, weeeeeeer
squeak and clankle
snow's been falling
my breath steaming
a car horn
talking across and laughter
            Forever trapped
within my racial
identifications
my identity
that is
            Joyous cries from
the ever changing flood of forms
multiply in the dawn
and come apart in steps
yet build to be torn
            Is it really blue?
            Was there ever anything
on the other side
of the word working saying
as if the practice of them
were all that this world
expects
            I'm actually quite wounded
            Daemon of wingéd relief
dropping down from the sky
becomes the master of a region
all regions become

a passing over
      I am nothing but
the clay and come from rock
the clouds move overhead
and my hands
are searching and then tired
and the pain's confusion
drives me thru the blood
      Some mind
needed here?
      It's the door that I open
to go into the kitchen
      "But psychoanalysis was also directly linked
to linguistic perplexities due to its own use
of symbolic structures."
      I had a dream about you
all of you, all
the ones I'd met
or heard of, and
they proved themself a fool
in the normal round of things
and so I was at home
within the news of my sleep
      It is locked away
into days of placid floors
and blanched walls of dry ice
which sail thru the wind
like a knife of balm
and boredom
      250 million people
for sure
stuck in hell
      What drops
from the voice
was a description
now is falling
from the drop

in our conversations
in our communications
          Pull up your trousers
the glass around you
convenience store
of a solicitous nature
affords itself
in the best-kept part of town
you can see, because you have eyes
          "Ultimately
thumbs down"
          Alone, alone
the sounds and
the sight which
is so bland and
makes me think again
          Footsteps on wood floor
          They've got one discovery
either invest the baboon blood
building immune system
or die from AIDS
an extensive international
          Radiator knocking
shadows of hand
a ink mark
a rumble
jangling
pen makes a sound too
          Chattering of his head
as if it is not I
who happens
          "Prestone anti-freeze"
          For all the benign poet seeks
the world has a steel boot for
          "Now the author himself remarks
that the resistance of intelligibility is
what prevents the total destruction of the message

by the phonic figure. So prose is present
at the very heart of poetry: 'In fact, the verse
is constituted by antinomy. For it is not
unidirectional; it doubles back. If it
were, it would not be able to carry meaning.
Because it signifies, it remains linear.
The poetic message is at once verse and prose.'"
      When does music
silence, beat and rest
conforming to any category
or is it forced,
molded, magnetized
by the imperative
      Blaring car-horns
non-stop
      You thought
the present
was yours
but she
thinks it
away
      When we meet
it's a physical space we punch
and discover and map out
the absolutes of our meeting
in the form of an isolated
individuated meeting
instead of the meeting of all
      No one
not one single
soul, anywhere
gonna help me
      What before
and now consonant
to the tv
"English..."
an interview

I come back to
it is here
             This is the strophe
"dance"
             Nothing you do
ever goes away
the way of swells
or path over trees
is the culmination
of this breath
connected to death
             "Huh?"
rubber, jeans
relaxing
yawning
wind and wind
             The call went straight
into my being
there to raise havoc
and I wrestle
             "Open house
sun"
and we're going
the water's running
the saw-blade's wheening
like they say a baby
they say a baby makes
wee-wee in the air
             Avoid the puddles
the little puddles of poison
identity forms
slowly all down to
events inside the reason
for this or that when
it is the world, continually
             Counting, stressing
it is a knife as measure

slicing
        Onto the screen, colors
credits move on
match is lit
music and a familiar voice
buttons, I see, on my vest
"Ararat"
        "This signifies as well
that the semantic aim of metaphorical utterance
does intersect most decisively
with the aim of ontological discourse,
not at the point where the reference
of metaphorical utterance
brings being as actuality
and as potentiality into play.
Finally, it signifies that this
intersection of the poetic
and the ontological does not concern tragic poetry alone,
since the remark in the Rhetoric cited above
extends to poetry as a whole;
it applies to lyric mimesis as well..."
        Any thought you have
proposes a way in which
to do something to be something
        A small beard
thrusts out from his chin
and his face is a painting
and a bird note pierces
his body of bones
and we see the spokes on the wheel
and the shadows in the creases of rock
        "That's him up there, eh?"
        I tried to tell my parents
so long ago now
that it is/was a disease
killing everything in its path
no career will out-smart

those simple but illusive comforts
      Now we're going upward
on the wings of insight
that sees far and wide
      Imagining the dreamscape—
the horror
of others I know
      Wedged into
and coming at me
the fine white dust
settles on my eyes
and contracts their lids
to pucker and explode
      Words reside
in that usage
all are beaten to
in advance
like Berrigan said
of the broken arm
      Ripping stickers off plastic
      "The last movie"
humming, legs
throwing a stone
a connection of times?
a white cross
kissing
hammering chinks
      Sometime
in the future
      It is the need
to separate, to let fade
and immerse
into the doubt
of being which is
heroism, or its seed at least
to descend into the suit
      Philosophy

is the memory
of the human race
falling thru space
      The freshness
of a lie
      Sometimes
I'm a partial phrase
      Signs of outward grief
directed at mankind
dangerously approach
from the caterwauling
neglected propinquity of
existentiales
not to be forgotten in the address
      "Second, as we shall see later,
this sentence-as-a-whole itself
has a sense and a reference.
'The King of France is Bald'
has a sense apart from circumstances,
and a reference that,
in given circumstances,
makes it sometimes true,
sometimes false."
      Rapacious, inane music
as the tv announces
and then a voice
and a wind, cooling
over my leg the pad
is written into
as into the world too
goes all that I witness
      All of man's industry
has been his heart-thump
from day one
      Everything she dislikes
she holds up for center inspection
in the discourse she most values

What one hears
I can't spell it
comes down thru words
coming from my mouth
THE mouth?
air conditioner
and an alarm
            One nice long
easy turd
fell out of me
            Is the night
reason's mate?
            Watching the chinese channel:
we need to get out, off, of this
damned story-line
forget it, combine it
anew, let it all
go away, reflex the now
and let the story fall
            Too many people
too many
keep coming
            Listening is boring
a plug's cord wraps
around on the wood floor
shuffle of papers
little sound
eyes on the same notebook
air compressor
            This life as thought, you know
is a prison, an absolute
jail cell, no way out
must play a part
in the theatrics of slavery
and the wheels of machinery
            A Ph.D. in this:
wisdom that contemplates

the anus and the cock
where all comes from
from one, shit
the other, seed
            A distant roar
banging on wood
now close the cat
becomes what writes
my hands with fingers
the grain of wood of a desk
and the sniffing nose of my wife
now breathes and clinks an ashtray
            Why would any virtue
live in the past
bone-skull
"...descended from ancestors
that roamed Gondwana..."
foot with creases
all this I trap
            Broken spine
of the notebook
a jet soars outside
vacuum cleaner
itchy skin
            I don't know how we
got here, but it's you
me, genitalia-rubbing
            "The image is simply carried a bit further—
instead of seeing it happen,
one is obliged to live in it or leave."
            Fear's depth
outside's possible coupling
will, in time, undo this spell
well in eye's mechanics
            Just some
labeled persona
eventually I'm

becoming, tho looking
for ways or
a way even
tho it's not right
but in dialectical worlds
      "Ever gentle
itty bitty brush"
        Relaxing into the hills
of the slow moving land
"The effort exhausted her..."
a jet or helicopter
a helicopter
"Now 2 points..."
grunt and chimes sing out
      Reflection in the waters
one dead and the other
empty reaches with an arm
into the glazed pattern
and pulls out a memory
dead haunting
his face of horror
      And there's the American flag
      The tired separation
the wheel enters
stuck in mud
must come from
a place beyond all places
succumbing being's bodies
to stay on its fray from fear
      Bretòn matched wits
with the world
and whose last
gasp over the boundary
of a class-consciousness
sputtered 'surrealism'
into a present-tense
      The thing is, these are

propositional in inviting idea
as opposed to catachresis solely
or itself solely
		This is
coming down now
the magic of spell
thru all time and space
containing time and space
then not
		Riding on the Q train
I find myself
scratching other concerns
as the wheels
of the window-film
present interesting
shapes that move
instead of NYCity
		Now is the time
to do it
		What did we see
we would think to be
insurmountable as now
thru-out it all
come to pass
		All the people come in
demanding satisfaction
		The tides of heavy water
move into take
the strap of leather
and wrap it around your wrist
have left to haul all
in the wake of its light
		No way mankind
gets any innocence
back or more
but thru lying
		Being is a trance

once lost
it ceases
      "Our 15th anniversary"
rain running over metal
creaking wood again
pings on metal
creaking wood
plunk plunk
hums some music
      That music be
to the scroll of sight
its bidden secret scent
and flight
      And now, thru the degradation
of pure elemental earth's wonders
must I face the degradation
of my senses in the name of my night-nurse
lovely whose cleanliness and care
vanishes and in a magic ritual
perforce into forswearing
again the like unto her forever
      She's as heavy
as a brick
shit-house
      The surging wind
thru dry trees
      "Clearance"
a fan blowing
and noisy
"scratch resistant"
      Again, for those of you
who followed not my program
I will re-enter:
media's model
the d, g, and b sounds
go to break up, attack
and practice cat sounds

sparring Eddy needs some territory-male
       Transferring all my thought
identity and potential thought
onto the bell of the closing doors
of the subway
as I ride home
standing up
       "But how to keep proportion
when the tele-techne-
mediative powers
can launch counter-truths
and truths, to un-do
any assertion, when
we have an obligation
to the truth?"
       What words
have lasted
do you know
they know
as if they are
the quantification
of jaws opening
       The radio says
confidence is down
       The gloom, dispelling
the gloom, as over time
in the gray matter departing
becomes this sight
gained in the activity
to write
       Closing the window
the wind and air
having finally
made its way in
to the apartment
       Tapping
the edge of the cat-bowl

The chip I dip
and shave away
from the curving bowl
the bean-dip
to keep it clean
a neat way of eating
            He throws down the coins
            That the mind
know its regulators
thru the muse of you
I enter an entry
            "Road Scholar"
a tape on the kitchen table
sounds from the round
a whistle
an errant flush stroke
a horn
            It's not fun
to grow up and find
all your knowledge
completely useless
in midst the people's
cool silence
            "Swimmer preview"
            Those girls
the time
of my hearing them
car slows
doors and a
train
(feet shuffled and thud)
            Softness
you can puddle
all the world in you
and still come back
to do it again
            The cat's eyes

intense on the birdies
       When it's fresh
then you can
move it
where ever
you want
       That his only life
turning upon the wheel
shackled at the wrists
and the middle
and the legs
his heart kept
inside the body
on the wheel in the cellar
       Running upward
chains and a chassis
gotta get ready to go
many leaves
a light hallway
a smudge on white wall
a bruised knuckle
       The far-reaching eye
of the first interpreter
sees in one something
its copula within
of his own power-store
       A poet writes
my accord's dissonance
reason's reverberation
tempting me seduction-wise
       "You listen to me.
You got to listen to me."
This is lyric poetry.
"...two voices in monotonous
strophe and anti-strophe:
two bodiless voices recounting dreamily
something performed in a region

without dimension by people w/out blood"
        Shouting in the bathroom
all the vitriol
the forbidden topics
will never be shown their true context
        Always to be sent
and ever to stumble
always to well and
gush until your heart
presses the pale locks
of a wooden stable-door
        Blue carpet
boot
black pants
creaking wheels
another sound
"It doesn't
happen overnight"
        Belch!
        There is a place inside thought
that is untranslatable
it own history
its own set of circumstances
its own reason, evolution
who's language beams out eventually
        The more people
you reach and who watch
simultaneously your art
the more realist
the perspective
        Never will I part
from this grave's crease
nor mark up time
with letters not tall-grown
on the tables of destiny
hanging in the windows of the west
where the light softly leaves

and the wind growls at its coming night
      Where is it coming from
the round ball that bounces
      Narration
always pretends
to be outside of
what is most vital
and in as much as
an act, not an action
a theatrics of substitution
      Hush he's not
to be disturbed
bundled over his
intense place of loss
and the heat of its
searching vein
      Don't waste my time
with small talk
all you and your five
friends that quick
curl it into letters
in columns that
make me look
greater or lesser
than I really am
      "I had no idea
you were so filled
with sexuality"
      Out of the drunken past
the source of all our
decision
such liquor was
will be
      A stuffed
spider
with black
felt

legs
           Looking to find the bottom
of what seems to be
a recurring situation
           "It seems to me time
to deny oneself the convenience,
which has become a business in thinking,
of lumping the whole of western thought
together under a single word,
metaphysics."
           Now I turn on as the
refrigerator turns on
"Tim and Beata" with a
pen squared line
or something like that
now falls the book's type
into view
           In a nothing grip
pulls me into it
all the source
to all my problems
           There IS an end
to all your torment
all the conjugations
of that torment
           "Plausible denial"
"I love my godmother"
"Intercom"
"Ask for Tod Thilleman"
picking thumb's thick skin
"Pages"

LEVEL TWO:
Toward An Ontology

The Master Architect has arranged horizons in a renewing design.

Robert Duncan
"Stimmung"

Being is a trance
once lost
it ceases
            I want to get at
the meat of these numbers
as if they were not merely
numbers, but pauses too
that open the imaginative distance
contained in the a priori fluid
of the mind's given property
            What is there
but thru aberration
of mind!
            Strophe, each
wed to world
outside now
not having any internal
organisms
solely the primitive
world
has spots, insects, sounds
            "Can you find
these things

in this wild
traffic jam?"
            This slow world
zapped with
the place of places
I keep thinking
no matter its content
is the world
            A horn, or strings
sonorous
in and out
            "...the cat sees it
for the games..."
            I want my own slave
            Walking
turning
past a plant
now into the room
thru the window
I see pencils standing
behind file folders bulging
            The truth
might turn out to be
nothing
            A large puddle reflects the sky
the fence and the trees
mirror into its smooth surface
the fence and the trees
            Wings of separate color
stained-glass wire mesh
veins of straight
cubes dark and big wood
one square a mouth
a mustache of leaves
with two lead points
            Why did I
go down

why
did the booze
have a moment
as if the world
were that moment
forever
               The expiation of guilt
and the wanting need to be guilty
               I'm on the phone
and the room is my job
               Because of my blue vest
those girls led me
all the way underground
to the deli restaurant
where I ate and am still full
               When that thing or phrase
takes over synapse space
in the brain contemporary
coeval to spatial relations
happens in the length
of the meaning of that
thing or phrase
               "...Those ladies
could be here any second..."
               The world words evoke
is the world the writer's been banished
toward
               In a nothing grip
pulls me into it
all the source
to all my problems
               He throws down the coins
               That music be
to the scroll of sight
its bidden secret scent
and flight
               He is glowing red in anger

the place is a lurid dark red
a deep emanation pulsating
within the stones and within
the recesses behind him
upon the wrack that turns him
and upside down his nose breaks
and the blood is hard to breathe thru
      Now I talk about
how I saw
how I saw
kept it in my ken
all these years
"1962"
      "If they want to
get a wild card"
      I'm actually quite wounded
      All the meddling
the others invoke
in the name of reason
not a wealth
but a tirade
against the hand of god
your god you gazer
into the depths of to find
      Eleven million people
on 50 square miles of land
and only 1 or 2 characterizations
emerge from it all
      The soft gelid urge
of the pliant vitamin
muscled and greased limbs
moving into light
obscured by soot and mortality
slow breathing in a bastion of sound
      "Is that ok?"
      A distant roar
banging on wood

now close the cat
becomes what writes
my hands with fingers
the grain of wood of a desk
and the sniffing nose of my wife
now breathes and clinks an ashtray
            Shade under my knee
is the world
my hairy legs
"Americans are deeply concerned"
            Concrete red ring
heaving coffee machine
illegible focusings
the mind chooses I operate
the world we fall into
the wood grain of the table
can hear a head
            We masquerade our knowledge
as something
we do not know
as if
            Don't make a home in the brain
no one wants to go there
            UNDER DURESS
IN THE CREATION OF MEANING
            I do not want
to deal with your damn family
week in and week out
that's not why I married YOU
            Clearly my coevals, being back
home here is the thought
of the light coming thru
those high schoolers
the only ones worth writing for?
            Now he's an old man
listening to her voice
coming out of his desires

and relieves himself
in the hatred she had and
gives to her old name a glow
that smacks another buddy
on the rump of his body?
              Plate-lets
clouding my vision
              After getting lost in the hospital
I'm now witting listening waiting
my number 4889 the food
and the music in my opening
christmas said the one woman
in the midwest they're different
inside my brain glass partitions
              The big, open
empty waste of her children
will not rise into
the free air of today
and so they will be family
and never anything more
              This is the history of being
told in a nano-second
as if it never mattered
as if all else than
mattered in being
for to be fully
              Soft but firm now
the spirit of poesy descends
              It's the kinda
person you are,
damnit!
              They/we by extension
have no use for
the inner goal of mind
except to pick up
sex partners
of years of schooling?

Why write anything
but the sound
and the air-like sound
and inside it the outside
has a human dimension
we have further to go to leave
            "Hence the elaborate construction
of a poem like THE FOUR ZOAS
gives way to the serial organization
of OF BEING NUMEROUS, the
individual segments refusing to
build toward 'Bravura Rhetorical Climaxes',
much less to comprehensive answers."
            "The closest Eddie Bauer store
is at Broadway & Prince
in New York"
            Joyous cries from
the everchanging flood of forms
multiply in the dawn
and come apart in steps
yet build to be torn
            My sleeping
heavy-breathing wife
            Don't waste my time
with small talk
all you and your five
friends that quick
curl it into letters
in columns that
make me look
greater or lesser
than I really am
            Trying to come down
from all the high
realizations
            Here come
the serendipitous

"Kwaytio Ki Mow"
water in the fridge
a carpet
lines running down
scrofula on my jacket
water in the back of the refrigerator
spots on the kitchen floor
lines running
          Old guy
sits next to me
in the mall
"I'm glad I'm not
long for this world.
I don't want to live
in a computerized world."
          Sitting digesting
what's the significance
of the turtle in the picture
of the meeting on air
which sings of a breath seen
and scissors its way to intention
an ambulatory reason no doubt
          "Language
spread into darkness"
          Footsteps on wood floor
          Did it all just
pop off and say good night
          Sound-bytes, commercials
speak to my soul
          "The deductive approach
(moving from general theory to
particular examples) is frequently
overshadowed by the need
to work by induction (from
the particular to the general)."
          North side of town
line proceeding in the mind of the

next line I'm writing we say
wind cold on ear
geese and birds fly this way
          "...the thing to do now
is to get you registered..."
he says as he comes to this
and begins to speak
hearing the footfall of the large
whirring air-engine in the waiting room
          I am a primitive
hear my cut-off value
waddle in the air
(they turn the radio on
downstairs outside in spanish)
          The history of being
human being
seems to be different
from the history
of the world, if indeed
the world has
any history
          And now, thru the degradation
of pure elemental earth's wonders
must I face the degradation
of my senses in the name of my night-nurse
lovely whose cleanliness and care
vanishes and in a magic ritual
perforce into foreswearing
again the like unto her forever
          There is a complex
inter-stellar mind
within the items
industry has produced
for human consumption
on into the eternal
matrix of the past, present
and felt equivocal strategies for being

Stories
continue
but what
is it
else?
Slates of old pavement?
What burns me up
is the adamant will
to argue or consent
the individual poses
and surrounds himself with
as if nothingness
were some sort of life elixir
Wood floors
big squares
the lines between
someone was talking
about the grid
last night
all over the world
Dog bite
and car honk
"...that shall enmesh them all"
What would a dash
do you think
serve toward composing
but the song
of human
her face
that jewish girl in
How ignorant
the people are
debasing eternal moment
in favor of the anti-logos
place where is channeled
much numb vibrating nothingness
Get it over onto yourself

by passing thru the dust
over and over again
my hand hurts
why is it always
to take time for me alone
my concerns are ridiculous
                So to the
wall of time
and more pieces
of these beats
who think or into thought
become the form of thought
then out into waves
of more of themself
more than thought
                Trying in my mind
but this mall I'm in the tiles
a voice and squeaks
are what I let myself become
in order to see into the coincidence
charging my info for what?
                It really does
pressure one to act
that's the way, the measure
the knowledge of all
the force thru the contrivance
to adapt, move, to be again
                Oh my god I
balling my head off
I'm all tearing and
gushing, it's
come full circle
the time of day, the end
the time of mind, the end
the end of the end: time to start over
                Wedged into
and coming at me

the fine white dust
settles on my eyes
and contracts their lids
to pucker and explode
        One nice long
easy turd
fell out of me
        When
the whistling
gathered in the pen
the forward march
of the sneakers
on the person
I can't believe it
        "...you can see it
travelling...word games..."
        I have people
that depend on me
strange to think
they could too be a part
of this empty rising head
of which I'm called
        All my youth melts
down into my inability now
        Something
scraped off
in, deep in the bowel
to show what motion
what release and everything to echo off of
forever and ever
        Enough energy
get it behind the thing
and push till you see
any sight at all as
the place that can't be named
        The primitive
realizes god is

not within him
but in the world
and great
                How do I remember?
                I have become the material
the MATER presence
all substance emanates
and have no earthly purpose
but the notebook I've carried
in my pockets of time
                Some things are fast some
slow and the slow is usually
the best like now again over
and over these strophes are becoming
outside my wish for them to be
a part of words in meaning
                "...Only if these drives are..."
wind thru the seed pods
wind-chimes tinkling
I am writing
my eyes blinking
notebook held in palm's crease
sound of the world outside this room's hum
                I had teeth
                ALL
marginal culture
in the future (from here out)
will be annihilated
by force (bigotry
will manifest as law AND object)
                Coffee cup with brown line
around its white center
a little handle like an ear
a gleam on a saucer
creamer pointed away
from me, a small cup with
sugar leafed out its top

You are not
going back in memory
you're going back
to the past
what it was, specifically
what it was as
something that is
          I return to the fangs
of a wild dog
mashed behind dark glasses
of a green rim
strapped with plastic
about its black sleek head
          The dream of a thousand dancers
escaping the blood
invading the world
with sperm's holdings
and no men
left anywhere to contain
their sovereignty and wield
          Via negativa
is called the way
called away
to duty
today
          You have the ability
to be prescient
but also scientific, empirical
which road will you take
and your voice the ultimate
guide/crutch?
          Is that
where I was always going to
the thing par excellence
there growing in a heaven
of hell indifferent
the people then came to mind

as the glue-buckets began to stink
       We don't know
but we're gonna find out
what poetry was, and
is, and, what's the difference?
           One thing's
for certain
trips in this day
to combine
             It is useless, pointless
to go on, even destructive
to go on, the wall
and the sky, and the things
are there, and there is no heart
only a large hole
           What young thing
silky black hair curled under collar
black tight pants made to flare
and those shoes there goes another
standing in the subway
cracks at my own shoes, count them
sounds of impending train believe it
             Are we always not there
and then decide to go
by car
to the hospital
and hear a truck
in the language someone's
trying to use
             Tv "calls from home
are one low rate
all the time..."
           The rain
I've moved into
with my mind
in order to measure
the motion of sight

it is coming down
      "...no mortar between them,
only a few verbs of being
remaining here and there."
      Plastic sibilance
      My identity
comes up on the screen
like an advertisement
      Conjugating
belongs to the human
realm
no language
at the helm
tho it (language)
is influenced
thru its manipulations later
      A pattern emanating
stick figures
hacking wacks of a snow shovel
finger on paper
computer hum
a whistle
series of ruffled time-pieces
"The box"
quotation marks
      To experiment means
to not give into meaning
and so all its components
are in continual process
of being re-used
existing in existence
hence the need to announce
ontology's foundation
      "...Action, doctor..."
      As the melos
drawn by the length
of blood and memory

begins anew
storehouse of knowledge true
            The horizon
is now at
the noon hour
we reckon by
hands
on a circular dial
            All these little things
trying to go thru civilization
the whole story
all these little things
clogging up the way
            Give me a cigarette then
            The burden of saying
anything at
release me
the water in the toilet's tub
the sound filling loneliness
that it matter only in my saying
anything at all
            Like the old stories:
you wander away
out from home
you get meaner
closer, everything
has a sentimental
apophansis, easy
            There IS truth
in advertising
don't sit there
with that
ancient
leftist glow—
life is life
            Notes
struck by the strophaic

echo all man's learning
and the aspirations thereof
      A grey sky
        Completely ruined
and out of breath
the seawrack about ankles
and the drifting clouds
come down over horizon
like they have
and like they must, still puzzling
        Energy
for humans
is all animal
sexual
engagement
or the possibility thereof
causing the corners of the world
to prick its ears
        This world is but
epidermis
for a deeper
truer
whatever word
sucking us in it should do fine
        Belly apple's fun find
to undo the mind of
sky-blue enhancement
falling from the history
the aeon of a dead year
bank's account finance moment
        This is the strophe
"dance"
        "Laboratory results
for Ron Thilleman"
far out, man
        Who were you vain
man to have killed

the most stimmung
thing-torch among
your species now
very very distant
       With your head
touching heaven
tending body burning
into the formless
sky's deity a multitude
have witnessed
until your non-emphatic day dawned
       Banana stems
blackly mottled
the print on the coffee cup
phone number
stove front
smoke
wrinkled clear plastic
"...iqui...tors"
"On january 28"
pen clinks, thrown
       I, poet, belong
and yet do not
having been cast out, and
forever doomed to wander
set my tent in what IS a desert
knowing no return but my own approaching death
       I am searching for knowledge
of myself and others
       Into the words
goes all my life's
young interest
       Please don't tell me
you want a
command
economy
       It is the power

and force of yellow
grape leaves changing
as is their charge
toward coming winter
      Wanting everything
to be where it is
for the composition
yes of course
that's what I've been
so preoccupied about
      Cat on my keyboard
rustle of matches
picking at my pen
rubbing
now on the leaves of paper
now back on the pen
      She's as heavy
as a brick
shit-house
      "Marble memo"
passing into
the toilet's sounds
the waves of grain in the table
the bars shading over the room
the watch on my wrist
      Empiricism
is always something induced
induction like a lawyer
combined with a nurse
combined with the law
combined with medicine, poetry
science of every man's kind
      Leaving the world
as the world
has left is gone
cannot
be anything other than

itself going to die
　　　　Mankind
seen from the historical
is all pomp, emptiness
and a foolish act
this moment could care
less about
　　　　　Avoid the puddles
the little puddles of poison identity forms
slowly all down to
events inside the reason
for this or that when
it is the world, continually
　　　　　Some people (most)
see language as a thing
totally unserviceable, unconnected
instead of a transfer mode
gets objects and those things
from there to here
from here to there, always
　　　　　Looking back
at previous utterances
the cat's toes clip on wood
the eyes blink
the shadow of my hand
and the ticking clock behind me
is the beginning of this place
or is solely THE place
　　　　　To write a congregation
of temporalities
　　　　　"Language really exists
only when a speaker takes it
in his possession and actualizes it.
But at the same time as the event
of discourse is fleeting and transitory,
it can be identified as 'the same';
thus, meaning is introduced, in its broadest sense,

at the same time as the possibility
of identifying a given unit of discourse."
   Leibniz and then
also Spinoza
monads and modes
"windowless cells"
said W. Lewis
they are already interlocked
in not being unified by Whitehead
and are called 'Reality"
   They pump those kids up
so high
they'll never come down
until they die
   I'm 17 years old
I'm looking at the library
I enter and
my life, the children
everything disappears
those words on a page
those poets and those books
wrap the afternoon in its strange hour
   There is no surface
or meeting place
for understanding
communication etc.
but all that works
thru rumor, intrigue
and mystery
whorls its rain into the ground
crops are vast enlarged land upon
   It's my own self's
my own enemy
   What is it
held in the palm of poetry
along the edges of skin
that pump full of blood

could make you over
in the blank face
of a relentless being
         Democratic vista then
we've come to understand
a multitude of sources
eclipsing the only source
         There are faces
we recognize
give us direction
and illuminate
every other dumb numb
piece of clay the world i.e.
         Growing wood water
rhythm walking we call feet
leaping synapse together grain
patterns I see metal
you see sand, the two
wherefrom come ye songs?
         Why do people think they have
a choice in the matter of who they
really are doesn't matter to the change
jingling now up out of the gullet
the body becomes a former thought
but without any other mind to think
or to light it becomes just writing
over and down to another line
the way we were tangent in school
         I sometimes feel
like my face and
being are composed
I let them compose
as an anti-thetical
being an alien a something
else besides myself
         The stupidity of everyone
I know is increasing

my blood pressure
          Feeling like I
should make monument
for some self
to call my own
show those byways
of the heart not transgressed
          "Honest to pete"
          Cacophonous voices
for a long time
          Is it all just
an ironic fervor?
          So
they've settled
on the terms
will take them thru
all their lives
no more discussion
no more other views
          "The last movie"
humming, legs
throwing a stone
a connection of times?
a white cross
kissing
hammering chinks
          You had idea
once, somewhere hip pocket
now gaining on
stellar opportunity
for someone else in
the far-flung galaxy of man
          No one's
going to be there
anyway
          All history
is momentary

You listen to all these people
you'll end up missing the boat
Transferring all my thought
identity and potential thought
onto the bell of the closing doors
of the subway
as I ride home
standing up
The air in my mouth
sounds like a wind tunnel
There IS
motivation
for everything
and it is
my own
self again
I gather
the limbs of Osiris
Cut them
all out
all off
cut 'em off
A voice, the roaring train
the pole in front of the woman
a space, an itch
another voice, under ground we go
her tits bobble, I can't
keep the pen clear-writing
Reading a book of poems
in the subway
I like to be noticed
and so does
the cat
the egotistically
sublime wildlife
has lived off my labor
for canned food

the world over
   Sometimes I switch
off the topic, the flow
too much, too fast
why?
   The thing that measures
is the large-in-the-small
the burgeoning unitary
"...from within..."
   Car and shower water
wafted in the bathroom
a ringing into my left ear
water just falling down now
script long lean and charging
   These midwestern
women are
wicked beyond
anything known
as wicked—
to know them then
their imperative geography
   "In the face of New York,
a voice of reason."
   Repeating myself
   It may be
the way you look
but it's certainly
an interface
a specificity
of sorts (whatever)
   Her ways
the ways of silence
   Mind-set that
made the strophe
now not the train
rumbling thru the station ceiling?
   Time distinguishes

what is practical
and what is not
in man's world
              This shell where my
ideas for thought's parameters
mutate I sound like something
via someone
hears when it wants to
and anticipates sight
              She's yelling at her dog
and pursues her own body
holds it that way
for a moment
whose arm comes to wave
and motion for his eyes to see
              When I think of them as coeval
they scare the crap out of me
              The end of a strophe
like the pain of writer's cramp
a car chassis squeaking
a bird on a quiet
morning street speaking
              Apparently
I can't get high enough
              Actors want to be
stars so they
can spend
every minute
observing themselves
              Gun, lines, gun
headband
blue lines
remote control
voices trapped me
              The potency of the world
language tries to harness
              What I wanna know is

how small can the heart get
how insignificant can you or them
or we become
before this whole thing comes to an end
       What is my body
but all my
hopes, dreams, aspirations
       Mosaic form moves
toward me
twinned by the angels
above faerys
to shed my eyes
into tears
my ears into wailing
       Daemon of wingéd relief
dropping down from the sky
becomes the master of a region
all regions become
a passing over
       History measures
from the téte a téte
       250 million people
for sure
stuck in hell
       Woman's world
a joke
an open mouth
nothing but teeth
in the act of
chewing more food
       Trying to be hip
by saying everything
as quickly as possible
       TV:
a commercial of pictures
a fade out
"Diane Keaton & Meryl Streep

concentrate on THEIR thing..."
        This train station
so insignificant
get my ire can't
rumble like that
departing train just does
take all its thought away
            At the possible confluence
the moist exciting
part of the game
            What is it that is so
pressure of the back
something between
pertains to what I've begun
to break thru to
what was never
fantasized about
something we're waiting for
            Blaring car-horns
non-stop
            Nature presents itself
from out of its own
perspective, not ours
tho we may admit
a parity to its wind
and change our view
            Books sold
movies sold
entertainment's an industry
from coast to coast
defining the inner lands
like cheaper dentistry in midwest
            Eye contact is
necessary?
            These amaranth branches
might indicate impermanence
I would need to direct

efforts in singing toward
the sky split by sonic sound
hammering the neighborhood with wood
from the contact of letters spoken
          Is it the pursuit of mind
the place that mind demands
or is it a woman?
          Strophaic
structure
is what I'm
in, me, must be
but it's a large spiral
beyond me, simultaneous
          My nails are getting long
so I jammed one bent it back
          Words exist at the level of
the imagination magneted there
by a bunch of shiny black
intellectual stares (stairs)
who knows who knows
who knows but breath
          She has to
go thru
the flames
          Apparently
there is a way
to turn on
and turn off
I've not found
without difficulties
          You tell by
the camera
          Sense guts beds flaps
rudiments guns fire sweat
tears blood cement goober
tongue-fire seminal injuns
rifle-carriers movement

firmament trepidatious
auxiliary mancillary mindful
            Streaming
idling is a name
to use to full
up the, this
time
            Loud gravel picks up these
people along the perimeter of you
            The sound of the world
is the lonely
trumpet sound of sex
            "Memo"
ashtray with 2 butts
folds of
cat falls off cushion
rain drops and pings of ice
pen, not my usual
the sound of the refrigerator
            "Caldwell, came in then
a little bit with his helmet"
            My social obligations
are not to speak of mind
until spoken to
then you can deny at will
following the sound of wind
falling in the world
            Coffee dripping down
into the dark glass-like
beads of responding
coffee
            A twenty and a five
dollar bill
folded together
            You can name sensations
as they come along they all
have fallen into something in

the words that's honeyed
by the sensation of the first
the most flush had us all
in the time of the human
            Are you almost
aware?
of what?
a mosaic?
            Knock your fucking wind out
            As if under water
all their (our)
language is
so communication-divers
must rescue sound
travelling slowly thru
that medium help us please
            Another young person
            The airplane over the city
now disappears
and so I begin again
my intention of delight
in the intellect of man
that simple mosaic
            Whole place of "zap"
when I look at
printed matter
            A profession of multiplicity
not repetition
but nature, the natural
which is the containment
of the symbolic
            Sentience:
marginal societies
viewed as inclusive
of the category
you're controlled by
its extensions all the way

thru the center of town
       "Life" could be substituted
for the most close-up thing
       I think my eye can
go anywhere it wants
only some places not
create those places it will
as bigger than when first
and also the not-seen
gets bigger
       Where is it coming from
the round ball that bounces
       Such a scandal
right in our midst
in our meetings
that can not
seemingly
be clarified?
       I'm not makin'
a goddamned
fuckin' movie, dad!
       What was I thinking
would connect
to this or that
and make sense
make my way
in the world
among the so-called people
       My wife is
shackled to a dream
she didn't authorize
       We are the animal
involved with nothing
but its machinery
since the beginning of time
nothing but tools
the proliferation of them

whirring in the air
humming work-tunes
      Empiricism
still munching
at the mythic biscuit
      Mind is the
danger
of continuing
in the mind
on the land
of ignorant monkey
      My rib hurts
from reading and watching
T.V.
      You can do
anything you want
that's a structure
within being
which is also a structure
THE structure of freedom
      If you think
of each strophe as a LINE
then you see
where it is loaded
      Human time-line
as a mechanism
beyond him
      I am guilty
for going against
myself, everything
I would have otherwise
set myself to do
and yet I see no other way
but this in which to thrive
      The freshness
of a lie
      Reflexive capability

my two hands in health
have nurtured insight
to this tree made to be
a bench in the mouth
of my mind I sit on
        We've heard rumor
of a place called thought
        I pull
out my little
penis to pee-pee
and think of
Ronald Johnson
author of ARK
        When I write a strophe
I'm trying to change the molecules of
my inner attachments to the world
so that the world and this engagement
become the most vibrant force
the most attractive among a host
of forces
        Too much talk in the world
and not enough poetry
        I need to reach
for my stranded self
constantly to be inside that some
or errant sight
        Y'ain't strong enough
to hold my love
and run with it
but I'll try
to give it you
        How grows that
girls face
she wants
to look
        To read
is to read all life

as the text at hand
        The violence
of my own hand
the only pain
the only politic this land
will ever and ever succumb to
        Composition
is not all deduction
from form and content
but is also and more importantly
induction
"longest play from scrimmage this year"
        We have resolved
to write no
event that hasn't
happened
        The burden is buckets
on backs and in stomachs
buckets of wind
the doctorate in cap and gowns
toothless and hoary
bitter and frail
        We've established
a quantitative
verse
but are now
had pressed
to gather
phone transfer
        Coming in
voice over
train out
side out
side my body
says to say
what it heard
        How do the

voices change
and the apartment
become important
"hot copy"
          Women see us all together
men see us all apart
and that's a fact, jack
          Alan Davies says
he hates structure
because it don't do anything
is therefore invasive
and yet were he to pull
heaven down
he'd find it still, silent
"who is she?"
          No, Mr. Enslin
it's not about time
tho it's beginning
to look in here
like something
I made up
because of my
locus of self pursuing
          Everything's
bowing down
at the same
time now
as the flowers bow
          How many
how much
is it
that works
inside
to turn you
to/against yourself
to give it all up
          Man's empiricism

is a near-sighted means
to a far-sighted
much unknown goal
      In this world
there are established institutions
categories and things
humanity uses as its guide
no other mind thought
hiccup or bodily momentariness
will outsmart its progressions
      With an arrow thru my head
the twist and the turn-around
as if on bended knee
most would be meaningful
more than usual
      The pens in my briefcase
water going down a drain
birds squawking in the yard
a rhythm transposing order
a jet goes by in the sky
cans and other instruments clink
sight sees lines on paper
thump
      What fantasia
the ear to being
hears, our identity
helps find in the world
just outside our door
      If you lay yourself down
like bedrock
others will come
lay themselves down
on your bedrock
comfortably stealing your bedrock
      "..."metamorphoses," his
quaint 19th century way
of saying "chemical reactions." "

Faeryland
is a psychosis that lives
in the blood and the land
activated when the senses
come forward and the world is shed
in favor of the animation
inherent in thematic butterflies
          The thought of mosaic
negates itself
and the mind stands in a waste
unable to hook-up with the world
read word for world
          Far away, closing down
by coming into the
world of
always
saying significance
          The artist
always treated the engraving
that way, to judge
its being by the depth
of each groove
how much sweat and toil
connoitered its depth to be
exactly where it is
          "Subjectivity
tends to separate man
from man, objectivity
brings us back
to the mass where we begin"
          It's a slippery realm
and no one ever cared
beyond caring so much until
it hurt and beyond that
nothing but mind looking at crumbs
someone's left from eating
making a mess caring for clean

What has come about
as I go down
thru the length
of the sperm of my limbs
and the time of the world
the mortality of knowledge
          Is it just
the ear
I need
to fill
or record
what has
what is happening?
          All ways
the eye and its meaning
crushing intent this
city's architecture
          "Have you ever
seen yourself?"
more time goes by
"I feel really horrible..."
the tv is a machine
is this freedom?
          These are the peregrinations
of cat-piss
exhumed from the
sky's adamant jet
nails us to decay
like a mummy I had said
in my head of non-existence
          I want the cute
girl, at the register
but the other one
(also cute)
was helping me
the most so
what do I do now?

White splotches
and the smell of paint
again with a brightness
and now we're falling
beyond where even
we should have fallen before
That me know
I see girls across the platform
rumbling wheels of a small cart
and the metal of a train on track
all said with a mind
never focused on the world
but is part of the world's power thru me
Why does my stomach
whenever I put
words coming into
my head just flow
whenever I forget
and go into the writing
as an automatic responsiveness

LEVEL THREE :
Toward An Ontology

.

The Master Architect has arranged horizons in a renewing design.

Robert Duncan
"Stimmung"

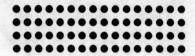

At this rate
it would be
about one strophe
every month chosen
with 300 notebooks
for the level the last
      Death – what they call
absence of body
      Clarity is NOT mind
but a worldhood
hooded in that.
Mind is the education
of ideation and citizenship
not ruled by
identity alone.
      Is that a part of
your identity
it is NOT
a part of your identity
      Going out of the way
into the painful isolation

sometimes thought
the pleasure of existence
but existence is not pleasure
it is existing
          "...which is the universe
coming into
its own universality..."
          How it is expected
you turn aside
from the daily stream
and make sense
tho it doesn't make sense
to anyone anymore
and they tell you this
          Gravity's
killing me
          Touch me feather of bright exchange
and tell if you would
all that otherwise will happen
and hold this up to purpose
steeled and resolute in columns of men
for the re-animation of a current claim
          What is it in the world
would highlight
on the coffee package
the world cold
and mean the world
for me at this moment
standing in the kitchen alone
          There is a place inside thought
that is untranslatable
its own history
its own set of circumstances
its own reason, evolution
who's language beams out eventually
          Surfeit, over surfeit
of being in culture

and no one, no one
knows what to do with it
      Scars on thumb
my head had turned
into the falling structures
of falling
in a world that fell
long ago
      What is it that locks me into mosaic
the anthropod's 'eyes'
un-free from the organicism of whole utterance?
      Is the totality of being
in my eyes?
      Joyous cries from
the everchanging flood of forms
multiply in the dawn
and come apart in steps
yet build to be torn
      Everything in prose or poetry writing
conspires against my original model
that view, as man
and so I continue
      It's not fun
to grow up and find
all your knowledge
completely useless
in midst the people's
cool silence
      Is that
where I was always going to
the thing par excellence
there growing in a heaven
of hell indifferent
the people then came to men
as the glue-buckets began to stink
      Some people died
and went into

the t.v. set
          The shadows
of the two strollers
like liquid ripples
over the sunny grass
late evening light
          Words contain
all meaning
in heaven
and earth
when you're
a character
out of shakes
          This, again
a beat
sustaining air of
words a-light from
back into deep meaning's well
the deep black
endless pit identity's
sucked into and covered by
          Source
to the reverie
source to the brain
          I miss my childhood's
neighborhood green
grass lawns
houses all
sleeping in
the america of
a perfect small world
          Please, who ever
can hear me
move
out of the city
go work in the country
to ballast the free side

what's left, of humanity
too late?
          Error causes
ears
open
lenses
make
a world
come home
          The suction on the peanut
jar sounds like memory
          Squeaking
and cruise now
clacking, a circle
squeaking and a rise
of turbulence
          Banana stems
blackly mottled
the print on the coffee cup
phone number
stove front
smoke
wrinkled clear plastic
"...iqui...tors"
"On january 28"
pen clinks, thrown
          Mind was
never more than
a visor's helmet
never identity
never cause and effect
but in history
which we have conquered
with the machines
          Out on the street
no life for a city
all the garbage I've been given

work my only retreat
          The mind or self
on its way to discern
comes upon a pause
with which the
force of all the living fills
from which our stories
have shapes
fearful and sinister
          I work
for the wallpaper
companies, and yet
my fellow "workers"
have no wish
to be associated
          By the light
of my penis
          Is it the wind
of one rumor after another
without regard
for culture, species,
identification
or ethical qualification?
          Cancer is not a feeling
but a cell disintegration
undiagnosed to the naked eye
          I want to get at
the meat of these numbers
as if they were not merely
numbers, but pauses too
that open the imaginative distance
contained in the a priori fluid
of the mind's given property
          What am I to do
search out people
just like me
make the same assumptions

live in the dark
a-more with them
            She wants
the end of the world
she wants it all
            Beethoven's #8th
the top of the theme
goes whirling like
an adamant disseminating
whirling spinning
heart of passion
I want
            It has such
rigid form
so exacting
that it has
no form
it is formless
            Blue vest
blue lines
energetic knuckles
the transfer
the train
            I've had enough of this yoke
going home to my woman
teach her continually
why to love means respect for me
            What IS meta physics
but 'idea' as it's
meant in the common reference
            Inscribed with
the expected
            The strophe must
present itself
as opposed to mind
asserting itself
            Unless I be unburdened

mistaken witness of flight
that burned a boy's
youth and married his station
with the tears of Beulah
whose huge margins
green the moss-banks of lake
titicaca
      The apophantic:
two surfaces that meet
are from inside man
one from outside
and they spectacle
in the baseness of is and is not
explained sometimes with as if
      What am I involved in now
as opposed to then
      Cut them
all out
all off
cut 'em off
      Slowly cutting
strophes into
the box
      Color as
primary
comes from
mosaic
and is best
explained there
      The world is
consonant
with the structure
of these strophaics
and may be
at any time
role-reversed
      Whole place of "zap"

when I look at
printed matter
        It is the cogito
on the wings of ZAS
and AHNAHR
as well as URIZEN
and LOS, and the sun
itself, we step into
become, and construct
a poetics, a poetry from
        A big ship
and everyone's a coward
to not step forth
and help its drowning hulk
dipping into the brine
higher each time over the top
        Is mother nature
alien like they say
to you're view?
        I'm not
something is not
allowing me
the written word to access
and maneuver
it for what
still comes to my chest?
        Gene fragments
        She did it:
Madonna made a fragment
walk and talk
the endless narrative
        UNDER DURESS
IN THE CREATION OF MEANING
        How can I live
anywhere but in
the mosaic THE
mosaic at all times

and as a result of
all action – yet
influenced its form to a high degree
by strophaic utterance.
      "New York"
fading
in and out
      Poetry:
there is no money in it
so no one therefore
will go to it
for ANY reason
      I am the thinker
and go deep
into crevice
that no one
even the owners
not want to know
      From supposed knowledge
to so-called animation
something's forgotten
a sentience, a knowledge
a part of knowledge
is left out and the fall
this then's the story again
      "...to thus characterize
poems trivializes
the whole poetic process."
      Taggart sees the
sound and to music
of poetry at war
with the ironic
interpretation that
becomes a whole person
      None of this that is
will be rendered
as nothing

by the future
of being
which collectively knows it
and looks for something else
something new that is
      I am the continual birth
of the little boy lost
      Again, for those of you
who followed not my program
I will re-enter:
media's model
the d,g, and b sounds
go to break up, attach
and practice cat sounds
sparring Eddy needs some territory-male
      Red glow
in the form of a question
bass filling my ear
the end is near
      I sometimes feel
like my face and
being are composed
I let them compose
as an anti-thetical
being an alien a something
else besides myself
      Too much talk in the world
and not enough poetry
      Mind hurts none but
sentence what? time
sight sound whirr does
there belly goes two
rise up O firmament
rise up from me
      WHERE
is the
eye

in all this
distant
land?
      You're never
gonna be able to get
your arms
      They produce
people like me
every other
blink snake summer
movement tune summer
inside vectors clicked
      A large puddle reflects the sky
the fence and the trees
mirror into its smooth surface
the fence and the trees
      Like the old stories:
you wander away
out from home
you get meaner
closer, everything
has a sentimental
apophansis, easy
      Some
thing
to say
here WAS
some
thing
to say
      "He was in luck; she liked
young men and she found
the idea of going home alone
extremely boring."
      Because she will substitute
any belief for the belief
called for

no belief is good enough
builds on nothing for nothing
and so we sit and wait
as if something different will arrive
          Knowledge itself
is an error
a scar
that will/must
one day be/exist!
          Milk bubbling
from the heat
the pan
          I'm 17 years old
I'm looking at the library
I enter and
my life, the children
everything disappears
those words on a page
those poets and those books
wrap the afternoon in its strange hour
          We can deduce
from language
AND induce
to our heart's content
yet what about THIS epoch
as opposed to that, or others
or me as opposed to you
          The notes echo in an anatomical
direction, thus composition
enters into stewardship
with the anatomy of being
          Follow
those things
around the
room, the
false soul
rays from it

you die not IN it
      Any thought you have
proposes a way in which
to do something to be something
      Everybody listens and learns
from Moira and her
emanation, about the
state, well, all they
go to do they
think is
there too
      Is it just
the ear
I need
to fill
or record
what has
what is happening?
      "The intriguing taste
slowly unfolds its mysteries"
      Metaphor, like the
French say
becomes DE TROPE
out of place
ill-consumed
by the knowing brain's senses
      The call went straight
into my being
there to raise havoc
and I wrestle
      You have something
on your mind?
then that's the world
a place in the universe
a galaxy a milky way
a traffic's engine sound
only in the world of the ear?

Teeth
while he's looking into the sun
        All those quantities
were s'posed to dissolve
into the running form
the soul over the world
running with the strength
        My pen is a clear plastic tube
describing or description as I'm
wondering in the bowels of the
state of things which is the
grammar or drug-raid heard
thru fear the mechanics of
language now married to flesh
        I have become the material
the MATER presence
all substance emanates
and have no earthly purpose
but the notebook I've carried
in my pockets of time
        How do you stay
and yet go out into the world
return home
        Doubt:
300 strophes
at one, right?
per three hundred notebooks
to be the final
selection of content
thrown into the
random hopper
        People think
they are the thoughts
but they refuse
to be and so
have mind
small under, themselves

Mighty thought
rises on the stem of power
          Mercy flows thru the land
as caustic as vituperation
in the high finance of self
along the border of eternity
within the sanctity of wedlock
for the arrival of the church
for the arrival of industry
          This positivity
is a charge
of negativity
when put
into duration's
spieling mind-hold
          You think
all this
pettiness
not
going to mean you?
          There is a complex
inter-stellar mind
within the items
industry has produced
for human consumption
on into the eternal
matrix of the past, present
and felt equivocal strategies for being
          I'm on the phone
and the room is my job
          You judge propinquity
by reason, what's
expected
          Sometimes it seems
I'm lost IN the strophe
and its total composition
does not illuminate anything

but that's the way I wanted it
and will probably want again
            We are all
trying to exchange that sticker
on the side of the
red plastic
milk crate
it's kinda illegible
having worn
over time
            Never will I part
from this grave's crease
nor mark up time
with letters not tall-grown
on the tables of destiny
hanging in the windows of the west
where the light softly leaves
and the wind growls at its coming night
            The mercy
of one self
one's own
private
history
Olson saw unfold
in the evolution of man
in the shores of the new world
            "The Admirals return home tonight"
the light in the kitchen
a cup of coffee
a hair under my left hand
as I lean on the counter-top
could be a code for women's world
but the tv is interrupting
            The world's
an adjustment
permanent of mind
hence body

must bear the brunt
of its rumored existences
       Grating
gum drop marks
a fire hydrant
feet with white shoes
this is my list for now
       This strophe
is also
an event
in the world
      Lexis=Bag
      They do not realize
that the change has happened
that the brain has been entered
and that millions of microbes
do not mean the same as they did
when they were in the world at large
      They are
trying to
find the
brain and
what it
does –
poetry DID
have measure
as sure as there WAS a world
      "Yet the red sun and moon,
and all the overflowing stars
rain down prolific pains"
      History as apophansis
the voice-over on the train
      Her eyes
pull apart the gloom
and all error and
its attendant rumor
run to

in the magic of ignorance
in the time of change
five worms on each hand
            Radicalize the talk
by eliminating ONLY
the political lie
            The radio in the morning
the cat's place
the notebook
held by the poet in the room
where his wife is laughing
his mind able to appreciate
all interpenetrations
            "...largely invisible
the enemy aircraft..."
            We have fallen
and we soar
as SEVLESMEHT
up against the helixed
sign of the air he
dreamt
            The absolute
negation
within the
potential
of the whole communal
of the people
            There are no comrades
in hell
only lovers
            "Why is it so easy to misinterpret
chemical and physical
occurrences with the process that is
being accomplished? These
conversations remind me of the
old man who tore apart a radio to
observe the transistors and studied

them for years until someone
finally told him it was not the tool
that made the music it was the artist."
          "Because there is no
known cure,
for some treatments
have potentially
serious side-effects"
          It is a philosophical liability
to see the beginning and the end
as one and the same –
without change mosaic rules
and a perpetual mentality
will struggle to side with change
wherever it exists, strangeness in familiarity
          "Swimmer preview"
          Crevice, secure light blindness
momentary gape in being
this or that revelation
related to non-being
it must be
for how else
would we think to act
but by holding it forever
          The radio says
confidence is down
          One stream of speech
but it's a host
a host-place of image
that talks, yes
but also radiates
the visible, AND
the presence of
          "The Numen Itself
shakes the very language..."
          Now
upon my return

searching
and releasing
not finding
what it was/
is, unless it's this
      Were it ever
to mean for us
then it's been gone a long time
      Hush he's not
to be disturbed
bundled over his
intense place of loss
and the heat of its
searching vein
      Getting to know
how my cursive
can be READABLE
      What would ever happen
but war outside love
      Transferring all my thought
identity and potential thought
onto the bell of the closing doors
of the subway
as I ride home
standing up
      "The picture shows (from left)
Igor Sergeyev, commander of the
Strategic Missile Troops, Igor
Rodionov, Defence Minister, and
Premier Viktor Chernomyrdin in
the command center of Russia's
strategic missiles February 21."
      "...working
for NYNEX
on video conferencing...
and interactive television."
      Will he ever

find the
golden
key?
          "Mrs. Hinkley
are you insane?"
giggles, giggles
"No further questions"
Salacious leg openings
"Perjury is a serious offense"
"They all know she's the murderer"
          I intend to be
the last man alive
so I can
have
all the women
coming in from outside
          "It is a problematic
of testimony and the performative"
          Access to place occurs
only after an "event"
and mosaic
is the only
event you'll see
outside your abilities
hence your goal
          All the breath of the world
driven into the unconscious
and the struggling epiphanies of the sub
          "It seems to me time
to deny oneself the convenience,
which has become a business in thinking,
of lumping the whole of western thought
together under a single word,
metaphysics."
          All culture is is
a generality
          Now the engine

stops and hums
as the space grows
and the head glows
I can see it
what miracle
what is happening?
            How grows that
girls face
she wants
to look
            The feral features
that can also look
wizened
            The rain
I've moved into
with my mind
in order to measure
the motion of sight
it is coming down
            Was there something
that brought me away
from all that
that people think
the way they do
still haunts my every move?
            Intake of air's my time
and only force's eye
compact philosophical statement
            Something in those combinations
not quite literary
but represent a future
that is and therefore
will be in the mind
of anyone who uses language
if only to speak with
            History's been subverted
by my ego-identificants

      The glistening
wet
cupboard
the tongue
touches
our world
      "...cannot be a systematic
study unless there is
a quality in literature
which enables it..."
      There won't be anybody there
to witness it anyway
      Here now comes no
breath will make it entirely
it does just speak it
talks of a being not all
mind but being inside
and being goes on and stays
and eventually goes
      We are the people
and we are revolutionary
and NOT
      I think he was
trying to
tell me
that we
share the same
woman —
but what does it
matter, man
      Poetry's given way
to philosophy
and philosophy
comes into poetry
all this by way
of being with legs
      Conversations

are like reefs
that should be avoided
by your vessel
you should have a vein
          Those two fathers
left their children
are now waling
over the field toward the fence
and the path
presumably home
          That poetry
has been invaded
by the psychologisms
of an unaware
class of specious
anti-beauticians
          Order shuffles feet
comes in to talk
under voice curves
from head full of
a forming mouth
          That dog barking
out there
for all I know
could be philosophy
          I know a people
who think they will be
or are found
within sex
but will never
let it all go
          Come with me
and we will see
the legs of the long sail-posts
reason themselves
into the sounding board
of the strophe-laden sea

That you or I
could do this thing
or any one
thing
so charges the strength
and weakness of mankind therewith
A rise
goose pimples
something strange in the moment
and the attendant event
How signs the static language
has become a visual part
of landscape technology
the eye following signs of language
over and thru the woods
to grandmother's house we go
As if there
were a
plate
in my
touch
Something deeper
than conscience
urges me on
Everything circles
into the eyes that take
the environment into
consideration, a summation
and every subsequent
ideation born to the lips
or the minds of us
are destined for that boring journey
Like Metcalf says
it is so large
when confronted
all plans for construction
melt and vanish –

thus I would address
you thru the COGITO
            They want
to act in a play
a movie
a radio show
a show which
shows nothing
            I came down thru the atmosphere
my head surrounded by atmosphere
the pressure unrealized until
            With Katya
with the trip done
my eyes glazing over
muttering something to her
where have we been
can we go there again?
            She doesn't WANT
to be known
and this causes
a re-occurring
problem
            I am in all
landscapes
            Don't waste my time
with small talk
all you and your five
friends that quick
curl it into letters
in columns that
make me look
greater or lesser
than I really am
            To win all life
within a form
make the form
and in its creation

the making coincides
with creation
      The pens in my briefcase
water going down a drain
birds squawking in the yard
a rhythm transposing order
a jet goes by in the sky
cans and other instruments clink
sight sees lines on paper
thump
      "...he memorializes
a sacralized time
through his behavior."
      Am I always in
touch with myself
when I drool?
      From concentration
into naming
it tends to promulgate
metaphysic
and not an
existential
      I keep chasing down
that horrible
emanation
from the world of people
who have gone into
the nothing of greed
without heed of need
      What now
better than a way
to know thyself
speaks from beyond the pallor
      Philosophy
is the memory
of the human race
falling thru space

One thing
rallies all the classes
of civilization
now, not to be
confused with
racial knowledge so-called
Look into
Habermas
on democracy
The ceiling bogs down
as it must for it is
the animality of a further
impasse, a gradation
toward the triumph
of imagination
gleaning the waves for succor
Speech the grounding
lesson of an entire
radius from here
Both to submit
and to rebel
If identity
has broken down
WHAT, if anything
can attempt to be
known then
and in what context
to effect consciousness
a commune?
Tapping
the edge of the cat-bowl
It's the fact of the proposal
that musters the words
into a belief construct
so it's really the continuance
of the fact the felicity of proposal
that elicits the erection within words

impregnating their ought silent wells
      IR36 strain
of rice plant
in soil yields
more upstanding
tons of FOOD
      The thing is, these are
propositional in inviting idea
as opposed to catachresis solely
or itself solely
      Thinking of the target
by feeling it in the center
of the burning red circle
goes thru my head like
two burning eyes
scared shown terror's door
the beginning of the end
      A new
notebook
will be needed
soon
the world
in all its
wave-glory-terrible motion
      As if my
ear were
all that
failure
      I am guilty
for going against
myself, everything
I would have otherwise
set myself to do
and yet I see no other way
but this in which to thrive
      Onto the screen, colors
credits move on

match is lit
music and a familiar voice
buttons, I see, on my vest
"Ararat"
            Something in them
makes them mad to know
nothing but what
they think they know
            All meaning
even exegetical meaning
abutts the great moving
wall of being which
is every where dead
and alive in a state of
ready participation in compulsion
            We seek a good stew
or broth that boils
in a nice contemporary
stainless steel pan
            Who are they:
you, the next one
extrapolating
the economy of
my own head which
ducks for the
gate's passage
            We would like our eyes restored
and our heads put to the test
our many muscles brought to bear
our life of living existence brought
into the folding verse of usage
more than usage the envelope
slips under the meter, is stamped
            Snow + fingernail
of Abwehr
a protean defense
protecting its essence

thru camouflage
layer upon layer
of flesh and meat
      The outside, the world
is now THE world
and my inner wealth of warmth
is dying against the length
and the night of ITS endurance
both?
      Distant reason
reoccurrence stop
eye-bean sucker
serendipity alarm
place outside
      Failure in strophaics resides in not
being able to disgorge as quickly as is
possible what is foremost in the writing
that place where all roads are
meeting like the end of the line
and the previous and the way you write
has everything to do to catch the flow
      I see you animated
and that is you
and this is me
where does right or wrong
come to play
where judgement?
      The world
is NOT
thru language
but informs
language thus it
always stands forth
clear and omni
unlike language ever can
      They put the needle
in the forearm of my father

so they can pump him
full of the stuff makes him
lose his hair
          Its issue life's issue
has always been choral
the rising harmony
or cacophony
of voices
mouthing their visions
or interests
          Wuzz after hope
americas fever-pitch
nothing gears home
words faces rearriving
dissembling assemblage
not satisfying in its coming
          Reflection in the waters
one dead and the other
empty reaches with an arm
into the glazed pattern
and pulls out a memory
dead haunting
his face of horror
          Empiricism
controlled from the death of the instant
the minute mind she warns
the faeryland fever reality knows well
the foundation of all hearsay
empiricism will not be able
to rest and then return with accuracy
          As the melos
drawn by the length
of blood and memory
begins anew
storehouse of knowledge true
          Empiricism, empiricism
knocking at the door

of my heart
and I let it in
      Any object
is the entirety of our languages
to have an earth of value
that echo again of the Olson ship
landing on terra firma
beats thru the blood of my time
      No one thinks
for themself
(or very few)
but it's the unconscious
making all the decision
casting all the characters
      furthering
my education
the sentence
is constructed
a verb
grounded in more
speech
      "The deductive approach
(moving from general theory to
particular examples) is frequently
overshadowed by the need
to work by induction (from
the particular to the general)."
      There is no knowledge
per se
within these
strophes brought together
but a being
whose strength
has not nor will succumb
to vain raptures
in a deathly lexical hell
      I opened up the deja vu

by returning
into the world
to find what I am
there and to find
that I AM there
       All poetry is thrown
into the encyclopedia's
furnace: 'he had
a musical beat
to his verse and it was
pleasant to hear":
nothing else happened.
       Is religion
the only path
mankind is on
is it god?
       The machine under the hummock of earth
bellows out from its confined
ever resurrected self-flagellation
where the cruel, the poor suffering
kneel upon bloody stumps
on a floor of vomited cement
       Rest is
the mosaic
but speeded rest
       Some guy just
farted in the
post office box room
has no place to go
but the fart does
he doesn't tho I'm saying
       "Perception is a prism
that transforms
the metaphysical world
into a physical world."
       Because the human
animal IS the judgement

of all, he rushes
to judgement, everywhere
he is the rush
toward liminality
   Apparently, all people met
indicate I
was not
supposed
to have made it out here
   A marching band
from Flatbush
into the
kiddy shows
of saturday morning
   There is no more
that will reach us
in here, we humans
having been into production
and not into reproduction
the natural world
will no longer return
   Forgot
what I wanted to write
this morning
now light skedaddles
across the car
as over the bridge we rail
   The neighbors are out
in the backyard playing
radio in spanish
I'm sitting in a chain
the phone is ringing
let me get it
just a minute like they say
   Turn that dog-page
falling into a
bark must

alarm bursts
a vein on my finger
says something
not meant to be
            People
are not using language
when they talk
they're using structure
great and small
            Rain drops on window
rain coming down
paper sounds against the book
the table underneath
sounds in the apartment
up above
            There is nothing
in the world
even if only
violence, it is
nothing, to mankind
nothing, nothing
            Poetry
is the music
of the fallen man
            How Ronald johnson
brings everything
into the one
whether ambiguous
or not
it IS
nature
            always
the sound of the traffic
it's always that there
            The sunshine
and the tubes of shadow
and the book which has shadow

like in language
we cannot go further
than the grammatical
construction an effort
to communicate what otherwise
may or may not be known
      Is this
what they liked me for?
      Are you, as they
the only ones
who exist
here, there,
anywhere?
      Having something I was to write
now not, now having left it
but being possessed with these
words I guess I'm not sure
I'm not really sure of a lot
want to be careful to record
      You're out of the book
so it's time, they think
to get in the good big book
but the measure crashing all around
is not in anyone's book
the human seed dead at birth
or growing in divine care beyond divinity
      "Ever gentle
itty bitty brush"
      In the one punch
over and over again
goes my life
into the punch itself
and I become
the curve of the punch
punch-drunk with glee
      Just offshore
of what you know for sure

the mosaic can be entered
where everything is
in relation to being
            I opened
to you, you
numbed me
by having nothing
to say or work for
that proved beneficial
now I'm out to erase you
            Time gone by
that's the depth
of the things we say
is what we're doing
            The sucking
shape this
mosaic has
lives most
in what is
appears
to not be – so its BEING measures
            Do we
present our design idea
to that mega-monied
company, or her
which one
won't leave us
empty, facing inanity
blind control of all historicals
            4 days of chemo
basically the same seat
I'm writing at
phone ringing
wood grain
            I tried to write
about the containments of the mind
and now we are

about to embark
upon a lifetime
of mindless way
      Reflexive capability
my two hands in health
have nurtured insight
to this tree made to be
a bench in the mouth
of my mind I sit on
      Head north sound
lines shadow north
logic flickers
succumbs bridges
moves world sounds
      "Eagle"
water running
fart, stripped shirt
boiling spaghetti sauce
folded sweater
below two legs
and lines running thru
a knock
      The dentritic
wood-brains
the country pursues
believe it or not
believe it, or not
      Literature, finally
thank god
shouldn't have anything
to do with the goddamned
so-called mind of man
      The gloom, dispelling
the gloom, as over time
in the gray matter departing
becomes this sight
gained in the activity

to write
                Abstract is not
the one solution
but in a mosaic
all life
has the daemon of life
to lean on
                I am the egg of the world
and will hatch
into indeterminacy
thru the machinery
of syntax
                I know people
who think the hole
they live in
should be glorified
instead of gotten
the hell out of
                I used to live
in the mind
now I live in
change —
think what you
like
                I need to reach
for my stranded self
constantly to be inside that some
or errant sight
                Everything's
bowing down
at the same
time now
as the flowers bow
                Where was youth
to have now its world
so beyond its
essentially

as if it never were
but only in dream
   How all things
enter my mind
for the will has set up
a house therein
and has told to commotion
hush for the silence
of the identity of parts
   Like those kids'
bike-chains
they're on a
path
   "MY calculations are just
as complicated, I'm
the only one who can follow
them and yet I'm
not particularly keen
on passing for a glory
of the nation."
   Looking for rest
he's found it the table
rocking from my body a bird
it squeaks the wind the sound
squeals high-pitched
wind with it now a fiction
conceit curls in my mind
the coffee glints and I hear
   Those two women
trying to fly that
kite, have no
working dynamic
of its flight properties
as if they've never
done it before, they rely on the wind
   We chase
paper's

formalities
for tax and law purposes
            He calls her on the phone
sees in her a future
non existent, all in his
mind not working properly
the language turns upon
confuses better judgement rules
thru ethical mythos
            Because we are nothing
we have fallen
even from the lord's
own mercy
which ran in these
woods, in these rivers
the spirit drained
into the will of evil multitudes
            All these
words just
a scoop of
head-mind
goes deep
each letter
the physical scape?
            Thinking cogito round
music holds sky forms
wherefor rocky instauration
connects wood sight plates
names the unique ear
            Stories
continue
but what
is it
else?
Slates of old pavement?
            You can do
anything you want

that's a structure
within being
which is also a structure
THE structure of freedom
          The acid etches
all the way to the bottom
of the bottomless
without warning
it eats away
at the place you hoped to live
          I am nothing but
the clay and come from rock
the clouds move overhead
and my hands
are searching and then tired
and the pain's confusion
drives me thru the blood
          Meaning has no books
no learning
it leans into the wind
moaning over and thru
these lines that
send away for wishful knowing
          Duncan
spells it
"salitter"
as if to make much of the junk
the placenta would be
the stress the compost heap
          I can see it on they faces
they can't read, or won't
literacy reflected so
so that: those awful
words they spit at me
made me feel special?

LEVEL FOUR :
Toward An Ontology

The Master Architect has arranged horizons in a renewing design.

Robert Duncan
"Stimmung"

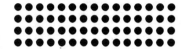

W hat bourgeois
crap!
            All voices
are
"crazy"
            What kind of
Dantescan discussion
of languae-lexical
meaning
suffices in this
atomic age –
anything but Beatrice!
            Getting to know
how my cursive
can be READABLE
            "...Those ladies
could be here any second..."
            They believe a lie
emanates from
the place
only words are
and not their disheveled
existential places

Where
out there
in all that
bad faith
can a human
parity and sentience
find expression
            Does it matter
if I say anything?
            It is becoming
increasingly difficult
to register anything
as very real
and not a total
theatricality take-over
            Knowledge:
the black
face
            Again with those
cut it out
do something else
            Is there belief
beyond knowing?
            What we are witnessing
is the world
entering our own
world
            Racial knowledge
encompasses
what is known
what is
familiar
            "Clearly
a better than expected
bottom line result"
            Because I
lingered I

thought too much
of myself
       The mind
as a chemical addiction
       We must now let go
and let fall to what
ever field or
category to control
       Clearly, words
are to be used for being
and nothing else
all individual identity
has been launched
       Empiricism (science)
tends to categorize
all sensate activity
under the horizon
of event
known as category
       "...the dialectic that reigns
between the experience of belonging
as a whole and the power of distanciation
that opens up the space of speculative thought."
       Is it
always different
or always
the same place?
       The only hope
is that she
discover
her relation-
ship
with father –
and yet what, now
does that mean?
       Where is it coming from
the round ball that bounces

There is a complex
inter-stellar mind
within the items
industry has produced
for human consumption
on into the eternal
matrix of the past, present
and felt equivocal strategies for being
            Oh their eyes
are empty
threatening
absolutely terrifying
            I feel lucky
a good thing for me
to have fallen
have the world
tell me how
ridiculous I am
            Here now comes no
breath will make it entirely
it does just speak it
talks of a being not all
mind but being inside
and being goes on and stays
and eventually goes
            Up, and
the space of sound
comes from what's heard
as if always
it sounds like
            It does matter
that you have eyes
and ears
and are using them
inside the age that
thinks for everyone
            How can

the strophe be
from first to last
the absolute
plenum of
the entire mosaic
      She has come
to swallow
ALL
      In a nothing grip
pulls me into it
all the source
to all my problems
      My father says
you're really good boys
really nice people
you don't deserve this
      "He had come on horseback
from Kentucky
and ended up with a
big spread
and a fine house."
      You say to
concentrate
on the work
but you refuse
to see how the work has ex-
panded as well, jerk
      In the middle
of my life
people
      "--the
images
in the catalogue
itself."
      I thought that if the
head were not dignified
belabored in that thought

then value had no name
and time needed throwing away
today I know, that short
unbecoming pang identifies
the hand fanning toward me, my only dread
                    Am I at the outgoing
of the intellectual spirit
composed of children's cries
newly conceived
from the round earth's
alembic of word?
                    Looking back
at previous utterances
the cat's toes clip on wood
the eyes blink
the shadow of my hand
and the ticking clock behind me
is the beginning of this place
or is solely THE place
                    The form reality takes
is the same form
the mind in reverence
in a conscious or
unconscious state has
for itself, has always
been, has not changed
but in its increase of frequency
                    To be released
into the strophe
to undo all linear
development
and build from
the world of one's own
thought, the world
                    We are placed
in a world where decisions
have already occurred —

any further so-called
ideation
must transpire on an
imaginary plane thus
feeding the real
          I think better
when I'm not thinking
y'all, dig?
          The verse is blank
because its quantity
is the call and response
of choruses
          Feet numb
a tape register
music overheard
shuffles
door flap
a sniffle
wood planks
whistling
          The worn
thread
of my sock
          Sun in the early
evening going
down slanting
finds the
building opposite
          Listen to me now:
being is a STRUCTURE
any thing that IS
          Children
lines going down the page
my balls tingle
a jet's sonic blast
continues thru the pen
          In this world

there are established institutions
categories and things
humanity uses as its guide
no other mind thought
hiccup or bodily momentariness
will outsmart its progressions
                    Interesting how
this strophe
when put
into juxta-
position
with others
it means
great gains for the mosaic
                    The talking on the phone
cigarette ash
when I look
"...flaky.."
                    "The face which
comes back in this
night of the earth
is a face from another world"
                    It's not just the one way
but THE way
glomms onto everything
the moment after you say
and to ask for help because of
is to bring in the world
and the world is vicious, no culture
to avoid it is really what you mean
                    What living matter
or is it mind
that is all of us?
                    When identity
is seen as a mosaic
some things come up to it
from the great mosaic life

and teach it that place
one would need to go on
        It's like starting again
and the streamers
"missing people..."
red glow from a couch
"get off..."
"I just can't help it, man..."
        One must
let the dusty light
come to one's eyes
and tell the world's fortune
in the glazing days of summer heat
before our time is up so
tripping to the field's high leisure
above the town –
all the clouds rain down
        Because she will substitute
any belief for the belief
called for
no belief is good enough
builds on nothing for nothing
and so we sit and wait
as if something different will arrive
        They want to
level everything
so that nothing
is what it says
        "They shot right
through the house windows
and exploded like fireworks
above the big tree."
        Was god a
trickster?
        I was always
incubating
meant to become

only thru that
period I
left myself
for dead
            Cat's greedily
eating from two bowls
            Held within the thrall
of imagination
there is nothing else
modernism's mistaken identity
a classical evolution
graces the world
            To actually
hear myself
complete a sentence –
have driven its
density within a grammar
toward the shores of
Gicheegumee (Beulah)
            I want to have intercourse
but I see
behind my eyes
now I'm hearing
now I'm the bell-tone
the siren breathing
            Our whole commune
is nothing but
the denial
of the elevation of speech
afraid of the height
are we
            Forget about trying to see sentience
as something to be gotten from animals
rocks or vegetables
and look into the humans around you
            To understand
means to

go thru that
wall
      Nothing out here
adds up to anything
      It's not fun
to grow up and find
all your knowledge
completely useless
in midst the people's
cool silence
      Doubt:
300 strophes
at one, right?
per three hundred notebooks
to be the final
selection of content
thrown into the
random hopper
      Radicalize the talk
by eliminating ONLY
the political lie
      Beyond
is it now
or now
or when
my hips
go up into the air?
      "The image of paving tiles
or of mosaic is deceptive
in this regard: words are not just
distinct from one another, that is,
defined only by their opposition
to other words, as are phonemes
in a phonological system;
they also trespass on one another."
      So, in order to
justify the mosaic

as a legitimate
structure for poetry
my culture has only one
prerequisite:
keep it sane?
          The life of the individual
is purely magical
the collective is hell
that seeped thru the cracks
          What is the mosaic
but my
contemplation
of its existence
thru deep time
(Duration)
          Mise en abyme
the picnic table
the crows
the pen writing
          When I broke
thru time
to be with
mind
I broke thru
all your
conjugations I now see
          To read
is to read all life
as the text at hand
          The mind is absolutely
ineffectual when
incoming
words that mouth had
worded
blasts it into blackness
a bleak survival ratio
unheard of in its reaches

Allen Ginsberg
just died
and I'm watching
the new rocket
shuttle blasting
off, his flower power
urging all humanity
in a contra-going
"Yet the red sun and moon,
and all the overflowing stars
rain down prolific pains"
You can
disperse, abstract
anything
"Parasites affect animals
and humans alike...
micro-organisms...
it's just that some battles
are more visible...timeless...
inescapable...a closer look..."
The assumption
that represents the whole
system
"...as their bases bit//
into earth..."
Our identities
have fallen into what
we know – and yet
again this happens
and happens
and happens
burning the very air we breathe
Too bad that
coeval male I
once met, who let me
be in his and her
company, has let

everything fall
to the body
WITHOUT mind or cogito
        Red glow
in the form of a question
bass filling my ear
the end is near
        Energy
for humans
is all animal
sexual
engagement
or the possibility thereof
causing the corners of the world
to prick its ears
        "...commenting on the revelation,
divides the whole book, as a tragedy,
into acts, distinguished
each by a chorus of heavenly harpings
and song between."
        Life has
faded from my mind
less there
less urgent
        The limits
of the garden
are the psychotropic
generation
sunk in deep dirt
that covers us
the living
        "The vision
was the color of my inner eye!"
        Mike-stands, knees
and cymbals gathering
all the force
a crystal candle yellow

red glow over the
bass yells
mouth black tonsils
          I as if had to
piece together
what came before
to what was now
a person complete
in that exchange
          Between the two great peaks
nature and man
we read with much
awe and reverence
the Ranger poems of Theodore Enslin
          Abstract is not
the one solution
but in a mosaic
all life
has the daemon of life
to lean on
          This space for sale
your ad here
call for terms
and financing 718-
398-9067 days
212-727-8170 neg.
          No longer
any objects to signify
          My mind
sees the end
and yet I go on
having to
and my mind
wonders why
          It is my identity
that has failed
failing, writing

the thing that is
the world
(which means
different things
to different people?)
            All my strophes
become a part
of the existence
of the mosaic
a place the mind
visits to survey all things
            "For a little time now
there have been three of them."
            When Heller (michael)
says he's
full of doubt
these days
does he
mean he's
full of feminine
objection?
            So many books
I haven't read
surround me every night
            Blue vest
blue lines
energetic knuckles
the transfer
the train
            Stanzaic, strophaic
breaking into line units
will want to be
put back together
or taken apart
            I have
learned how
to make it

squirt
            I will
eat you
out of house
and home
so don't
try to make
any point
outside that
realism
            You have something
on your mind?
then that's the world
a place in the universe
a galaxy a milky way
a traffic's engine sound
only in the world of the ear?
            Blood is
running in the
sound of memory
thrilling me
toward the release of sperm
in the eventual
future
of that feeling's world
            Light
on the kitchen floor
the things of this world
in a small space
our human glove opens
and closes and that's all
there ever will be
            The mosaic's space
is a performance
away from those who'd
like to pin it in a pine box
that is to say it's

humanly possible
          Her whole
hardship
really has
all the bearing
it so
sleepy and SUB - conscious
          Now the world
decides
for you
what will be
your place –
can you
admit
it?
          How "lonely"
Olson must have been
on his deathbed
reaching into people's
speech to grab
out the heart
always denied
          I keep going for the
sense impression
and it just depresses
me more
          I needed
order, even if it's
artificial, and so
found mosaic
and my attachment
is such
as to transpose into nature
          "It can also be
summarized as an investigation
of the relation between the ways
in which a society is codified

in texts as opposed to the
experience of individuals."
           Seems I was
just walking away from
school, only yesterday
short time ago, but I find
it to be lifetimes
literally, ago
           It assumes all
strophes
have the same
push
regardless
of their content
           Where ever I sit
has been
the hat like they say
does this make sense
what's it mean to make sense
(to complete something?)
           "...when you're nice
on the inside
it shows
on the outside..."
           If we find a path
to the mind
and sustain
a connectivity
will it matter?
           Olson wanted nothing
to do with politics
that took away
with the noise of
supposed ownership
the conspiracies of mankind
fucking too-loud non-music
           You listen to all these people

you'll end up missing the boat
          The cold vision
of contact
necessitates
a truth
whose worldliness
cannot but rule
until it melts
          There can be
no more political
talk about it
and so science
now comes to solve
all the socio-economics
thru an expanding
cerebral cortex
          What does it matter
what ELSE
you hear
do I have to
change you
thru your ear?
          Being is a trance
once lost
it ceases
          "Morphology, n. 1. the branch of
biology dealing with the form
and structure of plants and
animals. 2. the study of
patterns of word formation
in a language."
          We try to attain
to illusion
tho we are also
trying
to attain speech
with content

All the lights
went out
as I was
writing
poetry
        I want to get at
the meat of these numbers
as if they were not merely
numbers, but pauses too
that open the imaginative distance
contained in the a priori fluid
of the mind's given property
        "Because there is no
known cure,
for some treatments
have potentially
serious side-effects"
        It's all over
        How will
you explain
this energy
which is
the error
of life?
        When we go
we
let some words in
        There is
no foundation
in any discipline
or sport or work
or industry
it exists without mind
for the tyranny of rumor
wingéd daemon of nothing
        Everything
broke down

into the game
played by that loser
who cannot
believe a thing, and stands
forth before anything
takes place (me?)
            I am the egg of the world
and will hatch
into indeterminacy
thru the machinery
of syntax
            I listen and look
to the young people
surrounding me in daily
life's habits and habitués
and find that from early
embedded in their conscience
a form of giving and taking
not commensurate to what is said
            Looking to find the bottom
of what seems to be
a recurring situation
            The possibility
of this strophe
is harbored
within the moment
of the mosaic
            I see them spring forth
from the womb of earth
and carry out the grandeur
of spears and ropes
in the valley
of the many colored
sunsets
            The evident
area of the neighborhood
ruling all other regions

I could or would reach
by an annoying floorboard beat
from the downstairs neighbor's
stereo
    "I abandon the Dirty Inn
of my body, walled in
with flesh, reddened
with blood, covered with
hideous skin, full of
uncleaness; and, for my reward,
I shall, finally, sleep in the very depths
of the absolute, in annihilation."
    There were worms
crawling in the wound
from the blasted
war soldier's bed
eating his flesh
jaws he'd die to become
    "...you will
hear voices..."
    All the power
of the human world
exists in
doing time
putting up with
it in duration
    Try not to
be so
specific:
it always
means the end
    Some things are fast some
slow and the slow is usually
the best like now again over
and over these strophes are becoming
outside my wish for them to be
a part of words in meaning

Into the words
goes all my life's
young interest
These strophes prove
that the mind is real
at work in the world
I used to
roof it like they
say but
now I
hoof it
a simple thing
contains my way and all else?
Thinking of the target
by feeling it in the center
of the burning red circle
goes thru my head like
two burning eyes
scared shown terror's door
the beginning of the end
"Ever gentle
itty bitty brush"
Too much cowardice
when it
comes to being —
most people
unknown
to others
to THE other
coming to get them
Is there an extension of relation
that does NOT
have being as an invasion?
Time gone by
that's the depth
of the things we say
is what we're doing

Kripke insists, Rosemary
that there IS
a kind of logos
outside language –
but I'll be back in a moment
he says, I've got to do this
other thing, my science
. Touch me feather of bright exchange
and tell if you would
all that otherwise will happen
and hold this up to purpose
steeled and resolute in columns of men
for the re-animation of a current claim
I know everything
about it
all around it
thru it
and the sides
and how it comes
out in a form
that is it
There is a world
dying dying
unknown
dying unknown
Blue recycling bag
takes so long to write
the flowers have shadows
with cat-eyes of light
on table wood
sings like the birds
happy out back
The reified
value
from repetition's
dead something
now is the

door forced
open by its
non-mental brain-space
            The soldier shows
the young soldier
his place and warns him
to stay away
thus establishing an historical
the entrance to history that is
            Democracy IS anarchy
no evolution's involved
the only thing
that doesn't stay constant
is the population explosion
            Now
to the evening hours
the summer's
lengthening light
seems to say
            Watching the chinese channel:
we need to get out, off, of this
damned story-line
forget it, combine it
anew, let it all
go away, reflex the now
and let the story fall
            Under or around
the corner of structure
there is an
unforgiving place
instead
it should volute
and be forgotten
and fall to the designer
            Is it just a
selection
from the search

---

and bearing of being
that sums the being
pits it into lockstep
with the close and now, now
                What am I
creating?
                That me know
I see girls across the platform
rumbling wheels of a small cart
and the metal of a train on track
all said with a mind
never focused on the world
but is part of the world's power thru me
                Your idea
has a life
in life solamente
and not in reason
another day is coming
and that is the longevity
which boueys everything
                Is it something
in this world
is it of
this world?
                Sentience:
marginal societies
viewed as inclusive
of the category
you're controlled by
its extensions all the way
thru the center of town
                Horses of power
is that
what I await?
                The potency of the world
language tries to harness
                The sounds after the rain

the sounds
the birds
the little-ness
of every single
awakening under the light
            The women wish
to be co-opted
only by that with
strong physical
anthropomorphic
long animal powers
reaching into and riding
the emanation of the known world
            Something in them
makes them mad to know
nothing but what .
they think they know
            My failure to focus
and give to words
the reality I'm
in the middle of
            Pounding
in the other room
just like
Creeley's
visit to London
traffic of the
double-decker bus passes
            What from out the world
I pull into this paper
"...go ahead..."
follow your ear
footsteps up the stairs
            The people
are taken over by being
and it is there, or here
wherever it

really doesn't matter
but belief and identity
give way to
the march of event
an autonomous omni-relational
       I want only to enter you
nomenklatura
beautiful body
obsession beyond all others
beyond this human mind
sex sex sex
       "Good medicine"
smiling faces
letters on the page
hair on heads
person of the talking
container of knowledge
and/or milk
       Everything
and nothing at the same time
what fits on the line will and
the next line will also be driven
by the pen which I am holding
in a book that is on my lap
       Is the night
reason's mate?
       It's not just
an "historical
blackout" she practices
but a REAL
total black out
(now I HAVE
to live with her?)
       It is a philosophical liability
to see the beginning and the end
as one and the same –
without change mosaic rules

and a perpetual mentality
will struggle to side with change
wherever it exists, strangeness in familiarity
          Seismic
seismic
disturbance
          There is a place inside thought
that is untranslatable
its own history
its own set of circumstances
its own reason, evolution
who's language beams out eventually
          Searching
thru the subjective
for the objective
is a total
spleen and clownish
irony
never to be repeated
          From down there
they don't want speech
to make a language!
          A look
a feeling
brews their
whole life as
if life
were worth
just the duration of being
          Had I entered into contact
with something that knows
its way, and yet light
has ITS final say
for which I'm thankfully broken
at bottom and resign
to room toward this satisfaction
in the lee of its was and will-be

magical transaction
      Grasping onto this place
the sound of the fax machine
the radio, the voices
the radiator, the loud
punctured voice
a siren
      Why do you even get
warmed up
they're just gonna tell
you to go home
      I'm not
something is not
allowing me
the written word to access
and maneuver
it for what
still comes to my chest?
      People look different
than who they really are
      New York City –
I literally did NOT
understand your STARE
      Nothing
terrible nothing
is going thru
the bodies
every day
      "Language really exists
only when a speaker takes it
in his possession and actualizes it.
But at the same time as the event
of discourse is fleeting and transitory,
it can be identified as 'the same';
thus, meaning is introduced, in its broadest sense,
at the same time as the possibility
of identifying a given unit of discourse."

Daemon of wingéd relief
dropping down from the sky
becomes the master of a region
all regions become
a passing over
A raspberry
from the computer
Bachelard indicates
that psychology
induces a bestiality
because that's
all it de-
duces
Screwing
everything
into the wall
with an electric drill
"...they went up to heaven
and came down again
without recourse to trance."
Nature presents itself
from out of its own
perspective, not ours
tho we may admit
a parity to its wind
and change our view
Thinking seems to be a no-
brainer in that the world
appears and everyone in it and
then it disappears and there is
nothing to rely on and so you
switch it off like the nurse did
Enter into it
and change
They want
to act in a play
a movie

a radio show
a show which
shows nothing
          I can be somebody
to others
and another
to myself
          I got
everything
AGAINST you
coward individual –
grow up already
out under the only sky that is!
          Decrepit
as the script
this hand can
tell against
the outside
just now outside
now in the pen's script
          A receipt
sirens in a distant
blur of sound
now higher
and it is done
a single
rasping on gravel
          We are the words
we are the judges
          Something in my conscience
a beast I/we
could come up with
in bits and pieces
forever
this human limitation
each thought is
          Ripping stickers off plastic

The chords of the music
play over the afternoon
a silly song of sentiment
a dog barks to shut it
or to join
and the world turns
it's turning as I sit
slightly awkward on a chair
          Chattering of his head
as if it is not I
who happens
          "Yeah that's not a thing
easy to diagnose..."
"...and you want to go in in the morning?"
"So how many more kids do you have?"
          "There are powers"
the radio, "Bradley...
congressional...how much...
by the way...congress...
you may retire wealthy...
generous....corporations...
examining congress's pension plan."
          Speech the grounding
lesson of an entire
radius from here
          They think wakefulness
is the self that stays
ahead of the game
          The temporal
fold
IS
the brain –
you may
feel elsewise
but naught else
it is
          The freshness

of a lie
      All her fathers
have echo off
in the rough
and nothing
ever precise
      A mentality I alone see
but is mirrored in structure
one after another, next to
not impinging on one another
like the human world
      Fallen into their speech –
world, realizing poetry
and the word are a
difference of that world
within the sciences
of difference itself –
I have come to debunk
a limited use within being
      Once they get you
it's too late to get mad
you have to
power yourself forward
with nothing
(tho they'll find this out
too soon)
      "Having read your
terms of sale
I prefer to pay
by the following method"
      Like a small branch
a tree-twig
like the water
to get to it
infused
and also dripping
from it

from the whole tree
dripping in a wilderness
          "Life" could be substituted
for the most close-up thing
          To be
intelligent
not enough
one must have
contact with
what is
          Trying to find myself
thru the shifting stuff
of and on the mind of me
          History's been subverted
by my ego-identificants
          Europe was dead
by the time we
protested the plantation
of protestant ethics –
its vatican uber alles
and its migration of souls
toward procreation's hegemony
we bypassed for the indian's spirit-world
          "This registration period
lasts for
two weeks"
          My mind
is like the design
on that
bass guitar
          The frontier
is fraught
with a certain
cowardice
calling for
individual
despotism

            Who gathers
the mood
and slings it
toward happiness
frivolous ease
            And there's the American flag
            My method (like all)
poses an 'as if'
quality & quantity
of being that is NOT
being, but then
what is it that is, what
but a mosaic's distances
            The way
the way to go
is in the life
the happening
that is the event's energy
released into being
            Exiled
to the fucking
men's room
            It may mean something to you
but it's a waste of time
for me
            The distant land
across the wide water
not as then so
quickly traversed by helicopters
what to think but thought
useless human you have no world
but there it is nonetheless
            "Barracuda
Standard"
            Skunk mole spaghetti
a word in the mouth
insufferable ignorance

what sleep hose
it's all dead
            And if I can't
do it
then the view
from here
is
that it's totally
beyond us
            It takes money
to make
money: induction
is that
what we're dreaming
doing becoming etc.
            Before this happened
I was watching t.v.
and growing up in
wisconsin
            "But am I wrong..."
jagged black lines
got from "not
thinking anything..."
"I didn't..."
"Asinine..."
maybe not
            "Are there no stones
in heaven that
serve for the thunder?"
            All I want to tell you about
is that time on my way to
river falls wisconsin
I slept two nights
one on the train
the other all night
on trash heaps by the track-yards
freezing my ass in a northern snow-stop

Words
are the rhythm of stars
          The glistening
wet
cupboard
the tongue
touches
our world
          Mesmerized, mesmerized
mesmerized, mesmerized
          Her ways
the ways of silence
          Meaning is in the words
within their – my
lined shirt
black lines
and the white
like a milk
flowing between
          How do I
honestly
portray
myself
or any
self?
          Billowing violins
          Multi-
dimensional
(welcome)
mosaic
(but it ends)
          Some strophes get chosen
by the random hand
over and over
and find themselves
again in the land
of a speech-based poesis

streaming to sea
helped there by what
but the existence not presence of mind

Tod Thilleman is
Editor of *Poetry New
York, a journal of poetry &
translation*. He is the
author of *Wave-Run, The
Corybantes* (Spuyten
Duyvil) and *The New
Frequency* (Ma'arri).